FOOTBALL SUPERSTARS

Eli Manning

FOOTBALL ● SUPERSTARS

Tiki Barber	Joe Montana
Tom Brady	Walter Payton
Reggie Bush	Adrian Peterson
John Elway	Jerry Rice
Brett Favre	Ben Roethlisberger
Eli Manning	Tony Romo
Peyton Manning	Barry Sanders
Dan Marino	LaDainian Tomlinson
Donovan McNabb	Brian Urlacher

FOOTBALL ● SUPERSTARS

Eli
Manning

Ray Paprocki

CHELSEA HOUSE
An Infobase Learning Company

ELI MANNING

Chelsea House
An imprint of Infobase Learning
132 West 31st Street
New York, NY 10001

Library of Congress Cataloging-in-Publication Data
Paprocki, Ray.
  Eli Manning / Ray Paprocki.
    p. cm. — (Football superstars)
  Includes bibliographical references and index.
  ISBN 978-1-60413-753-8 (hardcover)
  1. Football players—United States—Biography. 2. Quarterbacks (Football—United States—Biography. I. Manning, Eli, 1981– II. Title. III. Series.

  GV939.M2887P36 2010
  796.332092—dc22
  [B]
                          2010019323

Text design by Erik Lindstrom
Cover design by Ben Peterson and Keith Trego
Composition by EJB Publishing Services
Cover printed by Yurchak Printing, Landisville, Pa.
Book printed and bound by Yurchak Printing, Landisville, Pa.

Printed in the United States of America

This book is printed on acid-free paper.

CONTENTS

1	Eli's Rise to the Top	7
2	Football's Royal Family	14
3	Eli's First Steps to Stardom	24
4	Eli Goes to College	33
5	A Rookie in the Big Apple	44
6	The Pressure Mounts	55
7	A Super Finish	66
8	A Hero Is Made	76
	Statistics	88
	Chronology	89
	Timeline	90
	Glossary	92
	Bibliography	97
	Further Reading	102
	Picture Credits	103
	Index	104
	About the Author	109

Eli's Rise
to the Top

The scene was soon after Super Bowl XLII in 2008 in the Arizona desert. New York Giants quarterback Eli Manning stood on a stage on the field while confetti floated through the warm February air. He hoisted a trophy in his right hand while wearing a T-shirt and a cap with matching slogans: "Super Bowl Champions."

Just minutes earlier, Manning had miraculously escaped from New England Patriots defenders to heave a long pass to David Tyree, who made a spectacular catch—perhaps the most memorable play in the history of the NFL's championship game. It set up Manning's 13-yard touchdown pass that gave the Giants a 17-14 victory in one of the biggest Super Bowl upsets. The underdog Giants had beaten the undefeated and seemingly invincible Patriots. Manning stood at the center of the victory, the game's most valuable player (MVP) and a nation's new hero.

Manning knows all about being a football idol. His father, Archie, was a folk hero in college and a star in the NFL. His brother Peyton is considered one of the best quarterbacks ever to play the game. In fact, Peyton led the Indianapolis Colts to a Super Bowl victory the year before and collected the MVP title, too. In a touching scene after the game against the Patriots, Peyton visited Eli in the Giants locker room, and they talked about the game with big smiles, acting as if they were in the privacy of one of their homes instead of surrounded by reporters and photographers.

For most of his life, Eli lived in the shadows of Archie and Peyton. Although he was quite successful himself, football fans and the media never considered him to be on par with his father and brother. During his first four seasons in the NFL, he was criticized for his inconsistency, for throwing too many interceptions, for being too low-key, for . . . take your pick. New York is a tough town in which to try to make your mark. And there is little patience for making mistakes.

By winning the Super Bowl, though, Eli became a superstar in his own right.

His story begins in New Orleans, where he grew up the youngest son of Archie and Olivia Manning, who had two other boys, Peyton and Cooper (the oldest). Archie had a long and distinguished career, playing quarterback for the New Orleans Saints, Minnesota Vikings, and Houston Oilers. All three sons were talented athletes, although the family didn't push them to play sports (Cooper was a wide receiver at the University of Mississippi until health problems forced him to quit).

Eli grew up as the youngest, always following in his brothers' footsteps. He is different from his siblings, who are quite outgoing. Eli is quiet and calm. As a child, he also became close to his mother. Thanks to her, he developed an early

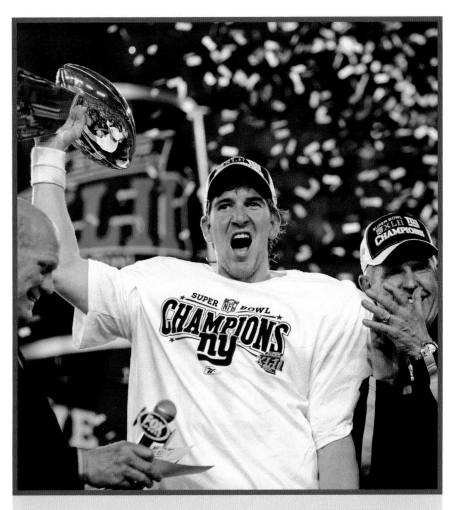

After leading the New York Giants to victory at Super Bowl XLII, Eli Manning was named the game's most valuable player. Winning the award and the championship game were enormous achievements for Manning, who comes from a family of football stars.

interest in antiques by joining her on shopping trips around New Orleans.

He attended the same high school as his brothers, who had made big names for themselves there. He, too, attracted a lot of attention. Newspapers from across the country wrote articles about the son of Archie and the brother of Peyton, who at that time was a famous college quarterback at the University of Tennessee.

The high school careers of Eli, Cooper, and Peyton left a big impression on their school, Isidore Newman. In 2004, after all three had long graduated, Newman retired jersey No. 18, the one worn by all three brothers in honor of their father's college uniform. Newman headmaster Scott McLeod told the crowd at the school, as a compliment to Olivia and Archie, "The person you are is the person your child will become." About the three sons, he said they had "set the world standard for behavior and grace. . . . They never put the benefit of fame before the value of friends." Cooper spoke for the family at the ceremony. In explaining why he was chosen to give the speech for the Mannings, he listed the accomplishments of his father and his brothers before saying with a smile, "but in the end it was decided that [the speaker] should be the most handsome Manning."

HEADING TO OLE MISS

Colleges heavily recruited Eli, and he chose to attend the University of Mississippi, just as Cooper and his father had done. Archie was a living legend at the school known as Ole Miss. You can't turn around on campus without seeing some mention of him. It would be hard for Eli to match his father's accomplishments there.

Ole Miss fans love their football. It has many rich traditions. One of the more popular traditions is the Walk of Champions, where fans line up to cheer the players as they head to the stadium for the game. Eli became quite familiar with the tradition during his college career—and also a bit savvy about how far some supporters of the visiting team might go. "It really gets you fired up for the games," he said. "You shake hands with people, you high-five the kids. I kind of hold something in my right hand just in case, a playbook or something, kind of do it all left-handed. You have to take care of the right, you never know. We might be playing LSU, and there might be an LSU fan trying to stick something sharp in there."

Eli got off to a rocky start at college. He was arrested for public intoxication during a fraternity party on campus. The incident helped him focus on taking his role seriously and trying to live up to his billing as a talented football player who was also known as a nice guy from a well-respected family.

After two seasons of watching from the sidelines, Eli embarked on a college career that would make him a national name. He took a struggling football program and injected it with fresh blood, taking the team to near the top of the acclaimed Southeastern Conference (SEC) and to its first major bowl in decades. He set a bunch of school records, breaking many set by his father. He was being compared to Peyton, who was already establishing himself as one of the best quarterbacks in the NFL.

In 2004, Eli was projected as the top pick in the NFL Draft. But then controversy erupted. Archie, who had spent a career playing for bad teams, and Eli told the team that held the top choice, the San Diego Chargers, that Eli didn't want to play for them. The Chargers had many problems, both on the field as a team and off the field as an organization. Eli's wishes became public, and many fans were upset with the Mannings for trying to get their own way. As it turned out, the Chargers did choose Eli but quickly traded him to the New York Giants. Eli was thrilled. But playing in New York, with its aggressive media and rabid fans, wouldn't be easy.

It was a big move from New Orleans and the small town of Oxford, Mississippi, home of Ole Miss, to the Big Apple. In fact, Eli wasn't interested in living in Manhattan, the heart of the nation's most exciting city. He bought a condo in nearby Hoboken, New Jersey, because it reminded him of Oxford in some ways. In fact, before Eli left home to join the Giants, he and his mother shopped at a bookstore in Oxford to buy a set of books by a famous author from Mississippi, William Faulkner,

Manning's record as a college quarterback was impressive, and he became the top pick for the 2004 NFL Draft. Although he had a rocky start with the New York Giants, his Super Bowl win against the New England Patriots quieted his critics.

as a reminder of home. In Hoboken, he felt as if he could move about without being mobbed by fans.

As a rookie, he was thrown in as a starter midway through the 2004 season and struggled a lot, losing six straight games before winning the final contest of the year. Over the next three seasons, the Giants became a good team, winning their division once and going to the play-offs each time. You would think that would have pleased the fans and the media, but expectations for Eli were really high. His play was inconsistent, as he made one great throw and then tossed an interception. Many doubted that he could ever become more than an above-average quarterback. The criticism could have crippled him, but he stayed strong and remained true to his even-keel self, which came under fire, too. A familiar refrain was: Why can't Eli be more of an emotional leader?

Then came the magical play-off run and the Super Bowl appearance against the mighty Patriots. After that victory, Eli quieted his critics. He followed that achievement with more notable news. He married his college sweetheart, Abby McGrew, and collected a number of contracts as a spokesman for major companies. He followed his Super Bowl victory with his best season yet in 2008, leading the Giants to the play-offs again and making his first Pro Bowl (an all-star game).

Heading into the 2009 season, he signed a new contract making him one of the highest-paid players ever in the NFL. It isn't all about the money and the fame, however. Eli has also been honored for his charity work, most of it involving sick children. He spends not only his money but also his time trying to improve the lives of people not as fortunate as he and his family are.

Football's Royal Family

Eli Manning was born into football royalty on January 3, 1981, in New Orleans. His father, Archie, was a phenomenal player in high school in the tiny town of Drew, Mississippi. Archie chose to attend the University of Mississippi. This was in the late 1960s, when there was much strife in the country, especially the Deep South, over civil rights and the segregation of whites and blacks. Hate and turmoil simmered as the old ways were hard to change in places such as Louisiana and Mississippi. In 1962, Ole Miss refused to allow a black student to attend the school. The National Guard was called in, and riots broke out. The university and the entire state were ridiculed across the country, its people viewed as small-minded hate-mongers.

Archie came across as anything but. He was not only talented but also friendly and polite. He set a good example as the star of the Mississippi football team. The state fell in love with Archie. A song was even written about him, "The Ballad of Archie Who," after a comment by a University of Tennessee player in response to a reporter's question about facing the quarterback. (The player's response was "Archie Who?")

He was soon on the covers of national sports magazines. He played an exciting style of football, scrambling from defenders and either running for yardage or flinging the ball downfield. "Here was this gawky, young, red-headed boy who came out of the Delta with enormous talent that he used for Ole Miss and the state," said David Sansing, an emeritus professor of history at the university. "We were coming out of a bad time with an enormous riot and civil rights murders in the state. This was a mean and ugly place, and then Archie came along. He was Mississippi's own Tom Sawyer, and he gave us all something to cheer. He was so good, and best of all, Archie was a good kid."

By the time he finished at Ole Miss in 1970, he had set 27 school records. He was named an all-American twice, and, in his senior year, he finished third in the balloting for the Heisman Trophy, which is given to the most outstanding player in college football. Archie was such a legend at the University of Mississippi that the speed limit on campus is 18 miles per hour—after the number Archie wore when he played there. Even with the accolades and achievements, however, Archie also had to deal with tragedy early in life. When he was a sophomore in college, Archie's father committed suicide after suffering from health problems. It was a devastating situation for a young man to experience. He wanted to stay home, get a job, and take care of the other members of his family. His mother, though, insisted he go back to college.

With the No. 2 overall pick, the New Orleans Saints selected Archie in the 1971 NFL Draft. The New England Patriots chose Stanford quarterback Jim Plunkett with the first choice. That same year, Archie married Olivia Williams; they had begun dating as freshmen at Ole Miss. She was a cheerleader and elementary education major who would later become a homecoming queen. "I knew Archie played football, but he wasn't on the varsity yet and I wasn't seeking a player," Olivia once told a reporter. "If I'd known what I was getting into, I'd probably have run for the hills."

He got big money, for that time, as a rookie with the Saints: $30,000 in his first year, which went up to $70,000 in his fifth year, with a $160,000 signing bonus. The Saints were an awful team, and the hope was that Archie would make them better. It sure looked that way after his first game as a pro: He ran for the winning touchdown to defeat a strong Los Angeles Rams team, 24-20. The team's improvement, however, was less than dramatic. The Saints finished with four wins that year, only two more than the previous season.

Even though Archie became a star, the team just kept losing. In fact, in the 10 seasons since the Saints started as a franchise in 1967, its record was 36–99–5. In 1978, the Saints had one of its best seasons, albeit still a losing one at 7–9. Archie broke through as a superstar that year, passing for 3,416 yards and 17 touchdowns. He won all kinds of awards, including the top individual honor in the NFL: most valuable player. It was a remarkable achievement because the MVP usually plays on a winning or championship team.

Archie had another strong season in 1979, and the Saints even won as many games as they lost, 8–8. The Saints returned to their losing ways the next few seasons, however, and Archie was traded to the Houston Oilers and later the Minnesota Vikings. In 1985, he retired from the sport that had made him a household name. He was more than an MVP and a two-time All-Pro. Archie also received recognition for his work with

In the 1960s, Manning's father, Archie, was the star quarterback at the University of Mississippi. Archie became known for his unique playing style and set 27 school records before being signed by the New Orleans Saints.

charity. He won two prestigious awards: the Byron "Whizzer" White Humanitarian Award and the Bart Starr Humanitarian Award.

When Archie retired, Eli was only four years old. He was the youngest of the three Manning boys: Cooper, born in 1974, was seven years older than Eli, and Peyton, born in 1976, was five years older. Like Archie, Cooper and Peyton were outgoing. Peyton was intense and serious. Cooper was the ham of the family, cracking everybody up with his jokes and antics. Eli, like his mother, was quiet and calm. His nickname became "Easy." Peyton and Cooper were very close as kids and extremely competitive. They also bickered, as many brothers do. Cooper remembers once when Peyton hit him on the head with a belt buckle and blood gushed out.

RAISING NORMAL KIDS

Unlike Eli, who was too young, Cooper and Peyton got to be a part of their father's career—playing on the field before games and hanging out in the locker room. Archie and Olivia, however, didn't try to mold their sons into athletes. Archie didn't care about them being football players. In fact, he tried to avoid talking about the sport with them. He wouldn't coach their teams and tried to stay in the background. (Although if they asked, he would show them the proper techniques of how to throw a football.)

He and Olivia just wanted them to be happy at whatever they chose to do. They raised all three boys to be humble and gracious. "They were taught to respect adults and have the right manners. All Archie and Olivia wanted was their kids to be normal. . . . The whole family is warm and generous, a joy to be around," said Billy Van Devender, who was Archie's roommate at Ole Miss and the best man at his wedding.

Archie and Olivia Manning bought a 5,000-square-foot Greek Revival home in the Garden District of New Orleans in 1982. The large house has been described as "elegant and refined, quiet and welcoming." Eli was two years old when the family moved in. The house had a backyard for the boys to play in, but a few problems did occur. "I can't tell you how many windows were broken in the house next door from our baseball games," Olivia said. Archie was still playing in the NFL but had just been traded to the Houston Oilers. The house needed a lot of work. "I told him, 'Just leave me a checkbook.' It probably saved our marriage," she told a reporter jokingly. Renovating a house can be costly and frustrating.

During Christmas, Olivia would decorate the tree with various ornaments, including those made by her boys, such as one with a picture of Eli as a first grader with glasses. When the children were young, the family routine for Christmas was to go to church on Christmas Eve, then have dinner at Antoine's, a fancy restaurant in the French Quarter. The family had brunch at home on the holiday.

Despite Archie's effort not to push his sons into sports, they naturally gravitated to playing basketball, baseball, and, especially, football. Instead of stuffed animals, a young Eli slept with Nerf baseballs and footballs in his bed. Archie encouraged his sons to play together in the backyard before signing them up for organized sports. In fact, there is a video on YouTube of the little Manning brothers in full uniform singing the national anthem outside their home.

Still, the three boys played a lot of organized sports when they were young. "Looking back, it seems like we celebrated every Fourth of July at a Little League tournament at Carolyn Park in St. Bernard, watching Cooper, then Peyton, then Eli play for Carrollton Playground," Olivia said. "It all started with baseball." Eli, meanwhile, was always the little brother. Eli "would try to play catch with Peyton, but he dropped too many balls, so Peyton took pillows off the couch and taped them to Eli's arms. He looked like a big marshmallow, but at least he could smother the passes."

But when Eli wasn't around his brothers, other kids recognized Eli's talent for playing football, even at an early age. As the story goes, when Eli and his fellow kindergartners would play football at school, he was chosen to be the quarterback. While

Eli enjoyed participating in sports, he also watched his brothers play in plenty of games. Sometimes he got tired of going, and Archie thought that, if they continued to take him, Eli might abandon sports. So on occasion he would leave Eli home with his mother, who would take him shopping with her to the antiques stores on Magazine Street in New Orleans. He wasn't

THE ELI FILE

Here are a few miscellaneous facts about Eli Manning:
- Favorite actor: Bill Murray.
- Favorite junk food: Pringles.
- Favorite TV show: *Seinfeld*.
- Favorite quarterback, other than his brother: Brett Favre.
- The Park & Sixth Comfort Food deli in Hoboken, New Jersey, offers a roast beef sandwich named after Eli.
- Unlike Peyton, Eli was not interested in learning sports trivia when he was growing up. So Peyton would pin Eli and hit him on the chest until he could name all of the schools in the Southeastern Conference.
- On viewing games with Peyton as a kid, Eli said: "Every Sunday, we'd be on the couch watching NFL football. . . . It was never sitting there talking, 'Hey, I want to be in the NFL and win a Super Bowl.' We wanted to win our little championship in our 7- and 8-league basketball tournament or whatever we were playing at the time."
- Peyton, Eli, and some friends took a summer vacation to Florida in 2003. Eli was still in college, and Peyton

interested at first, but over time he began to enjoy it. Even today, he has an interest in antiques, and he shops for them during the off-season.

When Eli turned 13, Peyton and Cooper were already off to college. He and his mother spent a lot of time together. Eli told a reporter that they would follow a routine of eating out

was playing for the Indianapolis Colts. The friends kept asking which of them could throw a football the farthest. So the brothers squared off and launched three throws. All three of Eli's tosses went farther than Peyton's.

- At the University of Mississippi, Eli was named to the Southeastern Conference Academic Honor Roll three times.
- Eli's first touchdown pass in the NFL was a six-yard toss to New York Giants tight end Jeremy Shockey (against Atlanta on November 21, 2004). Oddly, the first pro touchdown passes by Archie (to Dave Parks in 1971) and Peyton (to Marvin Harrison in 1998) also were for six yards.
- Eli, Archie, and Peyton hold a summer quarterback camp for kids called the Manning Passing Academy at Nicholls State University in Thibodaux, Louisiana. It started in the mid-1990s. In 2009, about 800 children attended the four-day camp. Some of the advertised counselors were 2008 Heisman Trophy winner Sam Bradford of Oklahoma, Texas quarterback Colt McCoy, and Indianapolis Colts receiver Anthony Gonzales.

Growing up in New Orleans, the Manning brothers were close, and they frequently played sports in the backyard and in the community. In this 1996 photograph, the Manning family pose outside their home. Clockwise from top left: Cooper, Olivia, Archie, Eli, and Peyton.

together once a week when his father was gone. With just the two of them, alone, they got a chance to talk about themselves. During those times, Eli learned a lot about his mother.

She grew up as Olivia Williams in Philadelphia, Mississippi. Her family's roots were as mule traders. In 1907, they settled in Philadelphia and opened a small mercantile store. Olivia's mother was quite an athlete, an all-state basketball player in high school. She was also the second woman in the state to get an airline pilot's license, in 1941. Apparently, all that athletic talent didn't come just from his father's genes. Eli has said on occasion that his mother is the boss of the family: "My mom knows how to do everything. My dad is clueless. I don't think he knows how to wash clothes."

Eli's strong bond with Olivia began when he was very young. He had trouble reading as a first grader. "As a child, it's embarrassing and frustrating," he said. "They call on students to read out loud in class, and it's one of those deals where you're praying the whole time that they don't call on you." So his mother would work with him at home. "Her laid-back attitude and her soft Southern drawl helped me keep calm about it. She's the one who kept telling me it would all work out and it did," he said. "Eli and Olivia are certainly very close," Archie once told a reporter. "They have that special bond that you see between mamas and their baby boys."

Eli's First Steps to Stardom

When Eli entered his freshman year at Isidore Newman, a small private school in downtown New Orleans for pre-kindergarten through twelfth grade, Cooper and Peyton had already made big names for themselves as football stars. Both brothers had been recruited to play at major colleges.

Cooper chose his father's alma mater, the University of Mississippi. Unlike Peyton and Eli, Cooper was a wide receiver. Cooper and Peyton played together at Newman for two years. In 1991, his senior season, Cooper caught 75 passes from his sophomore brother.

Cooper had a big problem in college, though. His hands were going numb. Doctors had a hard time figuring out what was wrong, and he suffered through several operations. Finally, it was determined that Cooper had a narrowing of the spinal cord, and he was forced to stop playing football. He didn't let that setback rule his life, though. He finished college, got married, became a father, and works as a successful stockbroker and as an executive in the oil business. Cooper continues to support his brothers by watching their games and keeping the family laughing with his upbeat attitude.

Peyton was a huge star at Newman, which is known more for its academics than its athletics. He set all kinds of records and established himself as a leader. One story that's often told is about the night Peyton won an away game in the last seconds and then exhibited his leadership skills on the way home when the team bus broke down. While waiting for help to arrive, Peyton took control. He played music and acted like a DJ, entertaining everyone until the bus was ready to complete the trip home.

By the time Peyton graduated, he was one of the top recruits in the country. He had plenty of choices and trimmed them to the University of Mississippi, the University of Tennessee, and the University of Florida. Unlike his father and brother, Peyton selected Tennessee over Ole Miss. His decision upset a lot of people in Mississippi. In fact, the Manning family received plenty of hate mail. Some of it said that Peyton was a traitor.

Peyton became a superstar at Tennessee. He was named the Southeastern Conference Freshman of the Year in 1994. After Peyton completed two more spectacular seasons, many people thought that he would skip his senior season and head to the NFL in 1997, but he delayed his professional career by one more year. He ended up finishing second in the Heisman Trophy contest and being selected No. 1 in the NFL Draft by the Indianapolis Colts, where he eventually became one of the greatest NFL quarterbacks of all time. He has been named MVP of the league four times and was also MVP of the 2007 Super Bowl, when the Colts defeated the Chicago Bears, 29-17.

The middle Manning brother, Peyton, was a star quarterback at the University of Tennessee. After college, he was drafted by the Indianapolis Colts, a team he would lead to victory in the 2007 Super Bowl.

ELI'S TURN

When Eli began his football career at Newman, expectations were high. Archie, Cooper, and Peyton had all become football legends by the time they had finished their high school careers. Could Eli possibly match or exceed their accomplishments?

Eli got his big chance when he was chosen to be the starting quarterback his freshman year after the first-string quarterback couldn't play because he had broken team rules. At first, Eli did not say anything to his family. According to Archie, "We're sitting at the dinner table, I think that Wednesday, and Eli kind of nonchalantly tells me, 'By the way, I'm starting on Friday night.' I almost jumped out of my chair." In that first game, with his nervous parents sitting in the stands, Eli fumbled once, but he also scored the game's only touchdown on an eight-yard run in the 7-0 win.

Another favorite Manning family story about Eli reveals why he earned the nickname "Easy." A few hours before the kickoff of a high school game, he placed a call home. His father answered and wondered if something was wrong. Eli asked for his mother. He wanted to make sure she would tape that night's episode of the TV comedy *Seinfeld*. Eli figured that Archie would have been mad at him for not concentrating on the game if he asked him to do the chore. "I don't know what I was thinking about. I think we were playing a bad team," Eli said. Those times when Eli did get upset or frustrated, he would play basketball by himself in his backyard. The basket was about eight feet high, so he would dunk the ball as hard as he could to release his frustrations.

It was clear early on that Peyton and Archie weren't the only talented quarterbacks in the family. Eli had the size (at 16, he was six-foot-four—1.9 meters—and weighed 180 pounds, or 82 kilograms), skills, and smarts to play the position exceedingly well. As a sophomore, during a game against Fisher High School, Eli dropped back to pass. Three defensive linemen came running at him. Most young quarterbacks might have panicked, either throwing the ball away, taking off running, or falling down. Instead, Eli stood his ground, looked downfield, and threw a 27-yard touchdown pass. In that game, he was 19 of 23 for 356 yards.

In 1997, during another game early in his junior season, he faked out the defense by slipping the ball to a running back, but he acted as if he were going to throw a pass. The defense followed Eli, and the running back scored untouched from 13 yards. Eli told reporters afterward that he learned the move from watching football films of his father and from playing with his brothers in their backyard. He also learned from listening to Peyton. "He's been a great big brother," Eli said, "and he's supported me in everything I've done . . . from being in high school, when he was in college, he'd come to practices and teach me the things that he was learning in college. . . . He didn't try to coach me on anything, but we talk football, we try to help each other out."

At the time, Archie said, "I worry a little bit about Eli. The word's out he's pretty good, and then that word becomes that he's real good, and then that becomes he's another Peyton." Reporters from major papers throughout the country traveled to New Orleans to write articles about Eli and his family. Eli didn't seemed fazed by the attention. "I'm easygoing. I think I can handle it," he said. Comparing Peyton and Eli, Tom Rushing, the director of academics at Newman, said, "Peyton, in many ways, was the most intense. Peyton was more likely to be serious about his studies, and his film-watching exploits are legendary. He would take home film. Eli comported himself much more quietly. The book was that Peyton was the better student of the game and Eli came with a few more natural gifts."

Before his senior season, college recruiters were swarming after him with offers to attend their schools. When Eli and his family returned home from a vacation to Wyoming, about 100 letters from college coaches were waiting for him. According to Tom Lemming, a highly regarded analyst of football talent, Eli was the fifty-ninth best high school senior football player in the country. He was ranked the ninth best quarterback. (He also was the only quarterback on that list to become a star in the NFL.)

Eli only improved his standing in his senior season by leading Newman to a record of 11–1 and the quarterfinals of the state championship. During his high school years, he racked up a bunch of awards, including All-American, All-State, and the *USA Today* Player of the Year in Louisiana. For his high school career, he was 429 of 725 (nearly 60 percent) for 7,389 yards and 81 touchdowns. He threw only 24 interceptions.

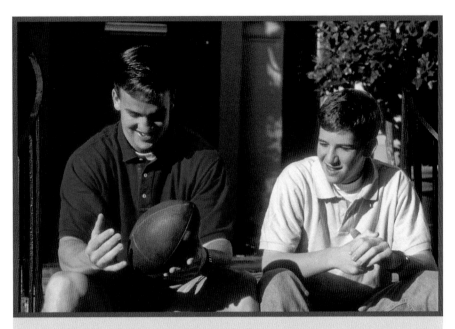

Eli (*right*) was a naturally talented football player, but he also credited much of his knowledge and skills to his family. Peyton (*left*) developed a close relationship with Eli and taught him the things he was learning in college football.

Eli's attitude toward being recruited was quite different from Peyton's. Peyton was very involved; he had studied the media guides of all the schools he was interested in to learn about their football programs. According to Archie, "Peyton knew about 300 [college football coaches]. One time, Mike Price of Washington State wanted to explain to Peyton that he'd coached Drew Bledsoe [who later started in the NFL]. Peyton not only knew that already, he knew the names of Washington State's first-, second- and third-string quarterbacks at the time." As for Eli, Archie said, "Eli knows of maybe 10 head coaches in the whole country, which makes him a more normal teenager." Cooper told a reporter that Eli got a letter from legendary coach Joe Paterno of Penn State and Eli didn't know who he was. Regarding the number of letters he'd received from college programs, Eli said, "I've been reading them and putting them aside for now."

On December 18, 1998, Eli sat at a patio table at high school while students looked on. His parents were there, too. He was ready to announce where he was going to attend college to play football. When the big moment came, Eli slipped on an Ole Miss cap. The winner in the Eli Manning sweepstakes was a

SERENA AND VENUS WILLIAMS

It is rare to find siblings as successful as Eli and Peyton Manning in professional sports. Perhaps the closest comparison would be sisters Venus and Serena Williams in women's tennis. They have dominated their sport since the late 1990s.

Venus was born on June 17, 1980, in Lynwood, California. Serena was born on September 26, 1981, in Saginaw, Michigan. They learned to play the game from their self-taught father, Richard Williams, while growing up in Los Angeles before moving to Palm Beach Gardens, Florida, in 1991 to train with other coaches. Richard, however, took the coaching duties back over while the girls were homeschooled by their mother.

Venus turned pro at age 14 in 1994 but continued to focus on her studies. Serena became a pro in 1995, also at 14, but didn't play much. In a couple of years, though, the sisters started to make big names for themselves. In 1997, Venus reached the finals of the U.S. Open even though she wasn't seeded. She was also the first African-American woman to go that far in the U.S. Open since Althea Gibson won the championship in 1957 and 1958. In 1998, Serena won the mixed doubles championship at Wimbledon with Max Mirnyi. The following year, Serena won her first Grand Slam title, at the U.S. Open.

school familiar to him, his father, and Cooper. The runners-up were Texas and Virginia. A big factor was the new head coach at Ole Miss, David Cutcliffe, who was the offensive coordinator at the University of Tennessee and had worked closely with Peyton. Of course, the Ole Miss fans were thrilled with Eli's choice. It was the biggest news since Archie had played there almost 30 years earlier.

Since then, the sisters, known for their athletic games and powerful strokes, have been at the top of the sport. Often, they end up playing each other in championship matches and battling for the top ranking. In fact, the Williams sisters have faced each other four times in the finals of the biggest tennis tournament, Wimbledon. Serena defeated Venus in 2002, 2003, and 2009. Venus won in 2008. Together, they have won four doubles titles at Wimbledon, the most recent in 2009.

Overall, Serena has won 13 Grand Slam titles as a singles champion. (The Grand Slam consists of four tournaments: Wimbledon, the U.S. Open, the French Open, and the Australian Open.) Venus has won seven Grand Slam singles titles. Eight times they have faced each other in a Gland Slam final, including four straight in 2002 and 2003. Serena has won six of the matches. Together, Serena and Venus have won 12 Grand Slams as a doubles team.

The sisters have made a name for themselves off the tennis court, too. Both attended the Art Institute of Florida. Serena has her own clothing line, Aneres, and has designed clothing for Nike and Puma. Venus is the chief executive officer (CEO) of V Starr Interiors, an interior design firm.

Again, Eli would be facing high expectations with comparisons to his father and Peyton. Still, Eli tried to downplay the comparisons. "I don't think I have to prove anything to anybody," he said. "The reason I work is to be the best. I don't have to be as good as Peyton. Sometimes you're not blessed with what people have. I want to play in college. If I get the opportunity, I'll play in the pros. But if something happens, injury or whatever, I think I'll be all right. I'm looking at a school where I can get a good education."

Eli Goes to College

When Eli started college in Oxford, Mississippi, in 1999, the town had changed a lot since his father's days. It had become more progressive. Students no longer waved the Confederate flag at football games. The town was enjoying an economic boost, with new restaurants and art galleries in the downtown area. Students were coming from every state and more than 70 countries, and, the student body was 12.5 percent African American.

Good things were happening, and one way to spread the word about those changes was by winning football games. A top-tier football program draws attention from reporters, who come to cover the games and write about the town. If Eli could win, the town would benefit. That's a lot to ask of a kid. "The really delicious aspect of this is with Eli you get quality, you get this personal package that projects the university, the town, and the state in a really positive way. Those are the two burdens in this, and they fall on the well-rounded shoulders of Eli," Richard Howorth, the mayor of Oxford, said.

Eli was ready. At his first press conference, he handled the questions like a veteran. Yet he couldn't escape history. There was the 18-mile-per-hour campus speed limit in honor of his father's jersey number. Inside a glass case at a sports museum there was a note of congratulations to Archie from President Richard Nixon. There was also the Archie Manning Room, with all kinds of memorabilia about his father.

"I understand the impact my father had here," Eli said. "I hope I can do some of the things he did. If I'm not an All-American or lead Ole Miss to a Sugar Bowl, I won't be disappointed in myself. I'm just trying to be the best I can be for myself and Ole Miss." Nevertheless, he also revealed that, behind that aw-shucks attitude, a fire was burning inside him: "If I'm going to do something, I want to know what's going on. I've got to be in charge."

Yet, doubts lingered as Eli began to find his way in a place where he would constantly be in the public eye. Even the pizza delivery guys would ask him for his autograph. "I was unsure of myself coming out of high school," Eli said. "I had doubts because of all the things that Peyton had accomplished. I didn't think I was as good as him."

Ole Miss coach David Cutcliffe didn't rush Eli. He red-shirted him as a freshman. That meant he was still on the team, but he couldn't play. Redshirting is a way for young players to learn the complex college game and not lose a year of eligibility. Eli spent the season working out and learning by reading his playbook and watching film of Ole Miss games.

As a freshman, he enjoyed his college freedom. He joined a fraternity, Sigma Nu, the same one his father belonged to. It was at a party held by that fraternity in January 2000 that Eli made

Although Manning was a successful high school quarterback (*above*), college-level football was a harder and more complex game. He spent most of his first year on the bench, observing older players and waiting for his turn.

the biggest mistake of his college days. The police were called, and Eli and a friend were arrested and later charged with public drunkenness. Articles about the incident appeared in papers across the country.

At first Eli apparently did not realize the seriousness of his mistake. When a campus officer arrested Eli, he asked him, "What do you think Archie is going to say about this?" Eli, making a joke regarding the song written about his father, said, "Archie who?"

He later understood that he couldn't be like everybody else and that his father's advice was worth following. "He always told me, 'You've got a name, people are watching. They want to see you mess up where they can tell the story. They want to be the one to walk in a place and have a funny story about you to tell. You've got to watch out. Know your limit. Know what you can do and can't do,'" Eli said.

Soon after, Cutcliffe had a meeting with Eli. He told him to think about why he was going to college: to try to become a star football player or to just have fun. Eli answered that he was serious about becoming a great quarterback. Eli began to work even harder and patiently waited his turn to play.

For the 2000 season, Eli, as a redshirt freshman, was eligible to play, but he rarely appeared on the field because senior star quarterback Romaro Miller took most of the snaps. During the regular season, Eli threw only 33 passes as Ole Miss went 7–4. Then came the Music City Bowl in Nashville, Tennessee, in December. Trailing West Virginia 49-16 going into the fourth quarter, Eli got to play. And play he did. In just one quarter, he threw for 167 yards and three touchdowns (plus an interception) to rally Ole Miss and give the Mountaineers a scare. West Virginia still won, 49-38, but Mississippi became excited about the next season.

ELI TAKES CONTROL

Now a sophomore, Eli took control of the Ole Miss team as the starting quarterback. The time he spent learning was ready to pay off. Excitement was high. The stadium was undergoing a 10,000-seat expansion, and a record 38,000 season tickets were sold.

It had been a long time since Ole Miss was anything special in football. Under legendary coach John Vaught, Ole Miss played in 15 consecutive bowl games from 1957 to 1971, which included Archie's career. After Vaught left in 1974, the Ole Miss football program had an overall record of about .500 and played in only a few bowl games.

Maybe things would change with Eli.

He got off to a tremendous start. In his first game, against Murray State, he completed 18 straight passes in a 49-14 victory. After seven games, the team stood 6–1. Ole Miss fans were thrilled, especially after Eli led the squad to a win over Southeastern Conference powerhouse Alabama with a last-minute touchdown. Just like his father . . . and Peyton.

Eli began to build his reputation for being cool under pressure. During a game against Louisiana State, on fourth and 10 from the LSU 30-yard line, Eli dropped back to pass. A safety was blitzing right at him. Still, Eli kept his poise and coolly found an open receiver for a 27-yard gain. "He held his ground and made a great play," Cutcliffe said. "When you are prepared, you don't have time to be nervous. You just play your game. He's a battler and a tough competitor." In the 35-24 win over LSU, Eli was 28 of 44 for 249 yards, with three touchdowns and an interception. Ole Miss looked like a strong challenger for the SEC West title.

Talking about both Peyton and Eli, Cutcliffe said, "Part of the genetics is what we see physically. What we can't see is the most gifted part, which is their ability to think so fast and formulate information into a functional ability to use it. They have great minds; they are great visualizers."

Then Ole Miss stumbled, dropping three of its last four games, including an incredible contest against Arkansas that lasted seven overtimes. Manning threw for six touchdowns and 312 yards in a 58-56 loss. At the time, the game was the longest in college football history. Ole Miss ended the 2001 season at 7–4 but didn't qualify for a bowl game. Eli had a terrific sophomore season, completing 259 of 408 passes (63.5 percent) for 2,948 yards with a school-record 31 touchdowns and just nine interceptions.

As the 2002 season began, Eli was considered one of the top quarterbacks in the country. In fact, many people were talking about Eli as a candidate for the Heisman Trophy. Archie, however, asked Ole Miss not to promote his son—to try to reduce the pressure on him.

Again, Ole Miss got off to a great start, 5–1, including a home win, 17-14, over No. 6-ranked Florida. Fans rushed the

FANTASY FOOTBALL

The story goes that Bill Winkenbach, part owner of the Oakland Raiders, and four of his friends, including two sportswriters, came up with an idea for a new game in 1962. It would be based on tracking the statistics of football players.

Today it is known as fantasy football, and it has exploded since the rise of the Internet to become an $800 million business. Studies show that 3 in 20 American men and 1 in 20 American women play some kind of fantasy sports game. That translates into millions of people.

For football, the idea is that a person chooses a team of NFL players—quarterbacks, running backs, tight ends, and wide receivers, as well as a team defense. Each week, the person keeps track of each player's statistics (plus the team defense) to build points in a match against another fantasy player. The fantasy season follows the NFL season. At the end of the 16-week schedule, a champion is crowned.

Some leagues are casual: a group of friends playing for fun or betting a small amount of money. Other leagues are more sophisticated and expensive, including some that attract thousands of people playing for up to $1 million in earnings. One league comprises 10 rich men who post an entry fee of $100,000.

Other businesses have spun off of the idea. Magazines and Web sites help fantasy players pick their teams. Companies sell trophies to league winners. There is even fantasy football insurance in which players pay a small sum to an "insurer" who will reimburse their league entry fee if a key member of the fantasy team misses a big part of the season because of an injury.

field after the game and tore down the goalposts. Yet Ole Miss, with a weak defense, stumbled badly through the toughest part of its schedule, losing five straight, including four on the road against ranked SEC teams.

It resurrected its season by defeating Mississippi State, 24-12, to finish 6–6. Despite the mediocre record, the team was invited to play in a bowl game, albeit a minor one: the Independence Bowl on December 27 in Shreveport, Louisiana. Ole Miss defeated Nebraska, 27-23, and Eli was named the Most Valuable Offensive Player of the game.

Overall, the season was a disappointing one. Eli threw for 10 fewer touchdowns and tossed six more interceptions than the previous year. The team's running attack did not help, finishing 110 out of 117 teams in Division I. Plus, Eli battled elbow and knee injuries.

The big question after 2002 was whether Eli would skip his senior season and head to the NFL. The deadline for college juniors to declare their intentions about the pro draft was in mid-January. Eli kept close counsel, but his parents, brothers, and friends had no clue what he was thinking. "Eli Manning is a different character," Archie said. "He listens. He hears. He doesn't say much. Eli would be a great poker player. He hasn't let his guard down for a second."

Projections had Eli getting drafted in the middle to late first round, perhaps the third quarterback taken, behind Carson Palmer of the University of Southern California and Byron Leftwich of Marshall University. Eli was already scheduled to graduate in the spring with a degree in marketing, so the only reason to stay was to continue to play football with his college teammates—and to try to improve his draft position the following year.

Eli decided to stay in school.

"I wanted another year of college football. I didn't have that good of a year last year," Eli said. "There were some things I felt I could improve on. I've only played 24 games in college. That's not that many. There's so much you can learn about defenses, about decision-making during a game. I thought I could become a better quarterback."

Ole Miss returned with 17 starting players, so there was optimism about the season. Eli realized that he had to step up as a team leader since he was selected as a cocaptain. Again, there was talk of Eli as a Heisman candidate, an honor neither Archie nor Peyton received. Archie's request to keep Ole Miss from doing a big promotional campaign in 2002 had back-fired. Eli was asked about his father's decision all the time. So this season Archie didn't get involved. Still, Eli was constantly asked about the award. His answer was typical Eli: "I never tell myself, 'I got to throw for this many yards because the Heisman is on the line.' If I win games and at the end of the season they want to invite me there, hey, that's great. It's out of my control."

Ole Miss got off to a slow start, splitting its first four games, including a loss to Memphis State. That defeat was particularly disappointing since Memphis State was not exactly known for its football program. The offense averaged 40 points, with Eli tossing 11 touchdown passes, but the defense allowed 44 and 49 points in the two losses. The fifth game was against the University of Florida on the road. The previous season, Mississippi had upset the highly ranked Gators at Oxford. While Florida was not as strong this season, it was still in the top 25 and revenge certainly was in mind. Ole Miss, however, pulled off another upset, 20-17.

The win over the Gators launched a six-game winning streak, the opposite of the previous season when Ole Miss started strong and then lost five in a row. Eli led his team to wins over Arkansas State and against SEC rivals Alabama, Arkansas, South Carolina, and Auburn. With a strong running attack, the pressure on Eli was reduced. He was more efficient, throwing fewer interceptions.

The University of Mississippi defeated Oklahoma State University in the 2004 Cotton Bowl, Ole Miss's first bowl victory since Manning's father, Archie, played there in the 1970s. Eli Manning contributed to three touchdowns and was named the Most Valuable Offensive Player of the game.

Heading into the next to the last game of the season, Ole Miss stood 6–0 in the conference—on track to win the SEC West division for the first time. Although they would be playing at home, the task would not be easy. The opponent was LSU, ranked No. 3 in the country. It was a tough, low-scoring game, and Ole Miss lost 17-14. Yet it rebounded to defeat Mississippi State in the final contest to finish 9–3 and 7–1 in conference play—good enough to be divisional co-champs. Ole Miss was invited to play in a major bowl: the Cotton Bowl in Dallas, Texas, on January 2, 2004.

At the Cotton Bowl, for the first time since Archie's team won the Sugar Bowl in 1970, Ole Miss won a major bowl game. Eli passed for 259 yards and two touchdowns—plus ran for one more—to lead the Rebels to a 31-28 win over Oklahoma State. Eli was named the Most Valuable Offensive Player of the game.

The victory ended Eli's career at Ole Miss on a high note. He finished with 10,119 yards passing—an Ole Miss record. He became only the fifth player in SEC history to throw for more than 10,000 yards. (Peyton had 1,082 more yards at Tennessee.) Eli also ended up breaking 47 Ole Miss records and picked up several awards, including the Maxwell Award for top collegiate player and the Johnny Unitas Golden Arm Award for best senior quarterback. The Heisman, however, went to Oklahoma quarterback Jason White, with Eli finishing third.

Eli also succeeded off the field. During his senior season, he was selected as one of 15 scholar-athletes by the National Football Foundation and College Hall of Fame. He was also a finalist for the Draddy Trophy, which recognizes the nation's top scholar-athlete.

Eli clearly enjoyed his college career. "I love Oxford. I love being in college. I love playing college football," he said at the time. "During the season, life is pretty simple, the same routine every day. Saturday's the best day of the week. I get to play foot-ball and get free time afterwards."

Now, Eli was preparing to follow an even more difficult path already traveled by his father and brother. It was time to head to the NFL.

A Rookie in
the Big Apple

Before the draft, college football players trying to make it to the NFL go to auditions called combines. All the teams are there to evaluate the players through workouts and interviews. Pro Days are smaller affairs, with players inviting coaches to watch them perform a series of skills. Eli held his Pro Day at the indoor facility of the New Orleans Saints. One NFL scouting report on Eli read: "Excellent size, good fundamentals and leadership skills. He is intelligent and makes good decisions. He has an outstanding arm and can make all the throws. He has good vision of the field and the defense, and is very accurate with a nice touch." The downside: "Not a great deep ball. Not very mobile. At times doesn't see the blitz."

"He's more athletic than Peyton," said John Dorsey, the Green Bay Packers' director of college scouting. "He has better feet, but he is not as cerebral coming to the line as Peyton. But Eli can make all the throws; his arm is alive; he is smart, and he is a Manning."

Smart, indeed. The NFL gives prospective pro players a test before the draft called the Wonderlic. It is supposed to judge a player's intelligence. Test takers have 12 minutes to answer 50 questions. The average score for a quarterback was 25 at the time (the test is also given to corporate employees; an average score for a lawyer is 30). Eli got a 39 on his Wonderlic.

Several other highly regarded college quarterbacks were available in the 2004 draft. They included Philip Rivers of North Carolina State, Ben Roethlisberger of Miami University in Ohio, and J.P. Losman of Tulane University in New Orleans. Still, many great college quarterbacks fail in the NFL because the game is so much more complex and difficult. Teams that draft quarterbacks in the first round invest a lot of time and money in these prospects. If they don't work out, the whole team most likely suffers for at least a few seasons. When it does work out, the team flourishes. It is a big, risky decision. Many thought Eli looked like a good risk.

Then a funny thing happened on the way to the NFL Draft in late April 2004. A soap opera broke out, with the Manning family right in the middle. It was an unusual situation because Archie and his sons rarely caused controversy or created drama, but this time they did in a big way. The first pick belonged to the San Diego Chargers, a team that hadn't made the play-offs in nine seasons and was also involved in a messy lawsuit with the city of San Diego. Eli did not want to play there, and Archie supported him. Archie, of course, knew what it was like to play for lousy teams his entire career.

The agent for Eli was Tom Condon. He contacted the general manager of the San Diego Chargers, A.J. Smith, with the family's news. "I got a call from Tom Condon informing me that Archie's wishes are we do not select Eli and he thinks that

New York is a good fit," Smith told reporters. "My response is I understand his position and his interest in the New York Giants, but we're going to do what is in the best interests of the organization." Some news reports indicated that Eli also preferred New York because he would have bigger opportunities to land endorsement contracts.

The Giants held the fourth pick in the draft. The only way Eli could play for them was if the Chargers and the next two teams didn't choose him or if one of them drafted him and then made a trade with the Giants. If the Chargers wanted to draft and then keep him, Eli decided he would not play. Instead he would sit out the season and enter the draft the following year.

Eli's idea of trying to force a team not to draft him was met with a strong backlash from football fans. The ploy sounded like the kind of thing a spoiled athlete would try. The criticism stung Eli and the rest of his family, who had hoped their desires wouldn't have been made public.

Draft day arrived on April 24, 2004, with the controversy still burning. Would the Chargers draft Eli? If so, how would he respond? Who would blink first? Commissioner Paul Tagliabue stood on the stage before the audience in Madison Square Garden and millions watching on television. He announced: "With the first choice in the 2004 NFL Draft, the Chargers select Eli Manning."

Eli did not look happy. The fans began to boo loudly. And kept booing. Eli walked on stage, shook Tagliabue's hand, and held up the Chargers jersey, but he didn't put on the cap with the team logo. The booing continued.

The Giants had the fourth pick in the NFL Draft after finishing the season 4–12. The team appeared in the Super Bowl just three years earlier, so the fall of the organization had been swift. The team needed a lot of help. Its general manager, Ernie Accorsi, wanted Eli as the quarterback of the team. The Giants decided to make a bold move to go after Eli. Accorsi contacted Smith of the Chargers, and the negotiations began. When it was the Giants' turn at No. 4, they took another quarterback, Philip Rivers of North Carolina State. The Giants and the Chargers soon reached an agreement. The Giants sent Rivers, along with their third-round pick and their first- and fifth-round choices in the 2005 draft, to the Chargers for Eli. That was four players for one. It was described as the biggest draft-day trade in the history of the Giants.

When Eli heard the news, he broke into a smile. "I admit I got a little worried at times," Eli said, "but I'm glad things worked out quickly. I didn't want to sit out a season. I wanted to play."

Although fans were still upset with how the Mannings handled the draft, the family did get support. "If Archie thought this was not a good situation for [Eli], his abilities— with him coming from the family tradition that he does—I would have been upset had he sat back and done nothing," said Kellen Winslow Sr., a former NFL star whose son, Kellen, was drafted sixth by the Cleveland Browns. "A father has to do what he thinks is best for his child. Archie is more qualified to make that assessment."

The reception for Eli at the Giants draft-day party at their stadium was quite different from the one at Madison Square Garden. About 3,000 fans cheered and chanted his name when he appeared on a stage in one of the end zones.

TOUGH START

While the fans were excited, those who follow the game closely know it's best to practice patience with a rookie quarterback. "Historically, when quarterbacks play the first year, they don't do very well," said Gil Brandt, former Dallas Cowboys vice president. For example, two great quarterbacks, Troy Aikman of the Cowboys and Peyton with the Colts, had lousy rookie seasons. Aikman went 0–11 and Peyton 3–13. In John Elway's first game as a Denver Bronco, he was benched at halftime after going one for eight with an interception. Elway, who

Due to the controversy leading up to the 2004 NFL Draft, Manning was booed when the San Diego Chargers selected him as their first-round pick. He was later traded to the New York Giants, the team he had originally wanted to join, in exchange for four other players.

became a Hall of Famer, later said, "I wanted to click my heels together and say, 'Auntie Em, take me home. You can have your signing bonus back. I don't want to stare at Jack Lambert spitting and drooling at me anymore. What the hell have I gotten myself into?'"

About 20 reporters attended Eli's first practice as a Giant in May. It was supposedly the largest media gathering for the team's minicamp. He didn't do well, dropping snaps and throwing poorly. The New York papers, known for their merciless coverage of the city's sports teams, ran headlines that read: "Manning fumbles his debut" and "Eli, Eli, Oh: First day a comedy of errors." Eli responded as expected. "I wasn't really surprised. I didn't let that get me down. I knew I didn't have a great first practice."

Peyton said he gave his brother the following advice: "Just to keep his mouth shut and don't go in there and talk about what you are going to do. Go in there and show them that you are there to work. You have to quietly earn the respect of your teammates."

Eli also had to deal with head coach Tom Coughlin, a hard-charging disciplinarian. "I don't mind being yelled at. I like being coached. I like a coach who's hands-on, who'll let you know when you make mistakes," Eli said.

The Giants dumped their quarterback of the past five years, Kerry Collins, and brought in veteran Kurt Warner, a two-time MVP who had won a Super Bowl. Eli would learn from him while competing for the starting position. The team got off to a good start with Warner at the helm, winning as many games (four) in just five contests as it had the previous year. But then the team began to stumble, losing three of four. Part of the problem was that Warner was getting sacked too frequently. Coughlin decided to bench the veteran. Eli made his debut as a starting quarterback on November 21, 2004, at Giants Stadium against the Atlanta Falcons, which featured a strong defense and its own young, big-name quarterback, Michael Vick.

When Eli found out he would be the starting quarterback, he again didn't tell his family right away. Archie actually found out from an ESPN reporter. When Archie called Eli, he asked him how practice had gone and Eli didn't say anything. Archie thought the worst: Eli had skipped practice. Then Eli said the team didn't practice on that particular day. It was another example of Eli having fun at his father's expense. "Everyone's always worrying about Eli, and he doesn't need it," said Merrick

Egan, a longtime friend of Eli's. "I think where it starts is that Eli kind of likes to toy with his dad," another old friend, James Montgomery, said.

Even though Eli was thrust into a big spot as a rookie starting quarterback, he would get little sympathy, especially

CLASS OF 2004

In 1983, three of the quarterbacks taken in the first round of the NFL Draft were John Elway, Dan Marino, and Jim Kelly. All are now in the Hall of Fame. Elway won two Super Bowls with the Denver Broncos. Heading into the 2010 season, Marino, who played for the Miami Dolphins, was the holder of 14 NFL records, including the most passing yards in a season (5,084). Kelly led the Buffalo Bills to four straight Super Bowls (none of which they won). Together, the three leaders threw for 148,303 yards and 957 touchdowns.

Three other quarterbacks were taken in the first round that year: Tony Eason, Todd Blackledge, and Ken O'Brien. Eason led the New England Patriots to the 1985 Super Bowl, O'Brien of the New York Jets was selected to play in two Pro Bowls, and Blackledge played seven seasons with the Kansas City Chiefs and the Steelers. The class of 1983 is largely considered the best crop of quarterbacks to enter the league at the same time.

The class of 2004, however, is making a strong challenge. Four quarterbacks were drafted in the first round: Eli Manning (No. 1 overall to the San Diego Chargers, then traded to the New York Giants), Philip Rivers (No. 4 to the Giants, then traded to the Chargers), Ben Roethlisberger (No. 11 to the Pittsburgh Steelers), and J.P. Losman (No. 22 to the Buffalo Bills).

since he had signed a contract worth $45 million over six years. Besides, New York fans and the media demand instant success—the same kind of success that another rookie quarterback, Ben Roethlisberger of the Pittsburgh Steelers, was enjoying that season. The eleventh pick in the draft was

The top three have emerged as among the best quarterbacks in the league after their first seven seasons (Losman struggled with the Bills and no longer plays in the NFL). Among Roethlisberger, Manning, and Rivers, they have set the following marks through the 2010 season:

- Gone a combined 184–97 as starters (Roethlisberger 69–29, Rivers 55–25, and Manning 60–43). As starters, none of their teams have had a losing record.
- Taken their teams to the play-offs 13 times (Roethlisberger 5 times, and Rivers and Manning 4 times each). In the play-offs, they have a record of 17–10: Roethlisberger is 10–3, Manning 4–3, and Rivers 3–4. All have appeared at least once in a conference title game (six appearances overall).
- Won three Super Bowls (Roethlisberger twice, 2006 and 2009, and Manning once, 2008) and lost one (Roethlisberger in 2011). As a comparison, the total Super Bowl record of Elway, Marino, and Kelly is 2–8.

Although the class of 2004 has a long way to go to match the career statistics of their counterparts from 1983, they are off to a great start.

playing a key role on a team that was on its way to playing in the AFC Championship Game.

Meanwhile, Peyton, who had signed a seven-year contract for $99.2 million in March 2004, making him the highest-paid player in the history of the NFL, was en route to setting a record for the most touchdown passes in a season with 49. (New England's Tom Brady broke the mark in 2007 with 50).

Eli got off to a tough start, with Atlanta winning 14-10. It got worse the following week in a 27-6 loss to the Philadelphia Eagles. Eli had only six completions and threw two interceptions. His coach didn't cut him any slack, telling the media that the rookie wasn't making enough progress. Fans booed him, and Eli's low-key attitude struck some New Yorkers as indecisive—not the trait people want in their stars. "I'm not the guy who runs down the field with his finger up in the air like I just saved the world," Eli said.

Warner offered encouraging words to the young player who took his job. "He's the No. 1 draft pick, and they put him in there, and everybody wants him to be a superstar. This team as a whole is struggling, and now he becomes the front man on that. And there are so many high expectations anyway, so many things based on his family name. He's going to be a great quarterback. But everybody expects it today. . . . It's hard because of all the things that come with it, especially in the New York market."

Eli played like a typical promising rookie. One moment he made a great play—a perfect pass for a 52-yard gain, for instance—and then the next he made a big mistake—an interception in the end zone. Eli lost the first six games he started. He looked as if he was overwhelmed. Playing quarterback is like trying to stay calm in a tornado. With so much swirling around, there is hardly any time to make a decision. Yet when the coaches looked at the game films, they noticed that Eli was making good decisions. Many times receivers weren't open or he was getting hit as he threw the ball. Still, Eli kept learning,

Signed by the struggling New York Giants, Manning quickly rose to the position of starting quarterback, but he was still an inexperienced NFL rookie. He lost his first game against Atlanta, was sacked by the Philadelphia Eagles (*above*), and his coach publicly criticized him for lack of progress.

even when his team was losing 31-7 against the Washington Redskins with only seconds to go. Instead of letting the clock run out, Eli called a time-out to get one more play in. One more chance to get better.

In the last game of the season, the Giants played the Dallas Cowboys. Although the Giants played better, they looked as if they were going to rack up another loss. Eli took the Giants down the field in the final moments. With only 11 seconds left, and the ball on the Dallas three-yard line, he did something that showed he was getting more confident as a leader. He called an audible, which means he looked at the defense and changed the play at the line of scrimmage by yelling out a signal to his teammates. It takes guts for a rookie to call an audible with the game on the line. It worked. He handed the ball off to running back Tiki Barber, who scored the winning touchdown. The Giants won 28-24 to finish the season at 6–10—two games better than the previous season.

"After the beating Eli took, he could not have ended his rookie year in a more upbeat way," said Ernie Accorsi, the Giants general manager. "The Cowboys go up three points with less than two minutes to go, and Eli marches us 70 yards. Not only that, he calls a do-or-die audible for a touchdown. That showed me something."

Although Eli's statistics weren't impressive—a less than 50 percent passing rate, and nine interceptions and six touchdowns in seven games—he did show steady improvement. He also survived the baptism by fire by remaining himself. About his biggest problems during his rookie season, he said, "It's the size of the defensive linemen getting in your face and forcing you into a bad play." As for any off-the-field concerns, he noted, "You're in deep trouble if you're on a turnpike and miss your exit. You may never get there."

The Pressure
Mounts

In 2005, as Eli began his first full season as the Giants' starting quarterback, the biggest issue concerned his elbow. During an exhibition game against Carolina, Panthers defensive end Julius Peppers hit Eli's arm as he started to pass. Even though he felt pain in his right elbow, he continued to play. After the game, team officials feared that the injury was serious and that Eli might be sidelined for a long time. Luckily, tests showed that the elbow sprain was not severe. He would be ready to play in the team's home opener. Eli commented that he was never worried.

Although Eli was not able to practice as much before the season began, the Giants got off to a great start, defeating the Arizona Cardinals, 42-19, and the New Orleans Saints, 27-10. That set up the game many people had been waiting for since

Eli was drafted. On September 25, the Giants would be traveling to San Diego to play the Chargers, the team Eli had spurned in the NFL Draft. The San Diego fans were still angry with Eli and his family. "People are pretty bitter at the family," said Hank Bauer, one of the Chargers' radio broadcasters. "It was a slap in the city's face."

In a twist, the Chargers had turned around their franchise in 2004 by going 12–4 to win the AFC West and make the playoffs while Eli and the Giants suffered through a losing season. The main story in the media replayed the draft-day drama, with Eli defending himself and his family. The sold-out crowd booed Eli from the start and only stopped when he threw an incomplete pass. Then it cheered. Early on, the game looked like a blowout, with the Chargers leading 21-3. Eli and the Giants could have wilted. Instead, they came back, closing the gap to 21-20 at halftime.

The Chargers, however, pulled away in the second half to win 45-23. The defense could not stop San Diego's efficient offense, led by veteran quarterback Drew Brees and superstar runner LaDainian Tomlinson. Eli played well, though, despite the raucous crowd: 24 of 41 for 352 yards and two touchdowns. After the game, Eli said, "I've had fans chant things at me before. So it wasn't hard to deal with." Eli earned respect from his teammates, the media, and NFL fans by performing well under pressure.

After the San Diego loss, the Giants split the next two games, setting up a home contest against the perennial powerhouse Denver Broncos, which were 5–1. It was on this day, October 23, 2005, that Eli made a big statement. The Giants trailed the Broncos 23-17 when they got the ball on their own 17-yard line with 3:29 to play. The previous week, against Dallas, Eli had thrown a touchdown pass with 10 seconds to play to tie the game, which the Giants lost in overtime, 16-13. Now, he began to work the team down the field again. First he had to complete a big third-down play from the 23-yard line, scrambling around before finding receiver Plaxico Burress to keep the drive alive. Later, he completed another third-down pass for 24 yards, putting the ball on the Broncos' eight-yard line. With only five seconds to go, and the ball two yards away from the end zone, Eli took the snap. The Broncos blitzed, and Eli kept backpedaling to give himself time to find a receiver. Then he fired a strike to Amani Toomer in the end zone. Touchdown. With the extra point, the Giants won 24-23 to go 4–2.

From there, the team won 7 of its last 10 games to finish 11–5, claiming the NFC East for the first time since 2000. Talk about a turnaround season. Although not everything went smoothly (Eli threw four interceptions in a loss to Minnesota), he lived up to the hype. "There's an inner toughness about him," said Giants quarterbacks coach Kevin Gilbride. "There's a resolve or resiliency that isn't immediately recognizable that allows him to get through some tough times, to keep battling and keep working."

In their first play-off game since 2002, the Giants played at home against the Carolina Panthers. The contest was a mismatch, as the Panthers won 23-0. Eli threw for only 113 yards and tossed three interceptions in the second half. Although the game was a bad finish to the season, there was a lot of good to look back on. The Giants scored 422 points, the second-highest amount in team history. Running back Tiki Barber was named the NFL Player of the Year by *Sports Illustrated* for rushing for a team-record 1,860 yards. Eli's 557 passes were the second-highest number ever in the franchise. He completed 294 of them, with 24 going for touchdowns—the most thrown by a Giants quarterback since Fran Tarkenton's 29 in 1967.

THE MANNING BOWL

During the off-season, Eli worked with his coaches to try to improve his play: He was aiming for a higher completion percentage and fewer interceptions (17 in 2005). Meanwhile, fans and the media couldn't stop talking about the game scheduled

Manning slowly gained the respect of his teammates and NFL fans as he continued to perform well under pressure against talented, strong teams. In 2005, Manning completed several important passes and defeated the Denver Broncos 24-23.

for September 10 at Giants Stadium. It would be the home opener for the Giants, against the Indianapolis Colts. Yes, Eli versus Peyton, or the Manning Bowl. The two brothers had never competed against each other, except in their backyard as kids. Now they would be the quarterbacks of two teams with big expectations following successful seasons.

As for comparing Eli and Peyton, there was no doubt who was better. Peyton, an eight-year veteran, had already won two MVPs and set the record for most touchdown passes in a season. But their 2005 statistics were not that different. Peyton completed a much higher percentage of his passes (67 percent to 53 percent), but they threw for about the same number of yards (around 3,700) and touchdowns (28 for Peyton and 24 for Eli). Eli threw seven more interceptions than Peyton, who had 10.

Their personalities certainly were in contrast. There was no question that Peyton led his team. The offense depended on his ability to call plays at the line of scrimmage, with him constantly pointing and barking out instructions before the snap of the ball. Meanwhile, questions about Eli's leadership persisted. Some members of the media wondered if the young, laid-back quarterback had commanded the respect of his veteran teammates.

Archie and Olivia tried not to make a big deal about the game when interviewed by reporters. "I'm not going to make it emotional," Archie said. "Both Olivia and I are nervous when we see our boys play. It's the big leagues, they play a tough position with a lot of pressure on them. I'm always nervous for them. I don't think I'll be more nervous because they are playing each other."

Still, this game obviously was different. In fact, it would be the first time in NFL history that two brothers started at quarterback in the same game. "I can't root for anybody," Archie said. "I wish they both could start 1–0. . . . The fact this was a goal they had, like thousands of kids, to play pro football, and there are only 32 [starting quarterback] spots and they've got two of them. I recognize that and I'm proud of that."

Eli and Peyton usually talk to each other on the phone on Friday nights during the football season. Unlike in the past, however, their chat before this game had nothing to do with the sport they play for a living. "We're afraid to say the slightest little thing about anything because you feel like the other guy is taking notes," Eli said.

Finally, the game arrived, and it was a good one. Both Peyton and Eli played well. Peyton went 25 of 41 for 276 yards. Although Eli fumbled and tossed an interception, he threw for 247 yards on 20 of 34 attempts. In the end, the Colts defeated the Giants, 26-21. After the game, the brothers met on the field and shook hands. Peyton said he told Eli that he loved him. "I thought Eli played his butt off," Peyton said. "He's every bit as good as he looked on TV, and he's going to be a great player. I'm proud to be related to the guy, proud to be his brother."

"A good game," Archie said. "I'm just glad I don't have to do this anymore."

IMPROVING HIS PLAY

The rest of the season for Eli and the Giants was like a roller-coaster: a series of ups and downs. The team got off to a 6–2 start, with Eli's best game as a pro to that point coming in a 30-24 overtime win against the Philadelphia Eagles (completing 31 of 43 passes for 371 yards and 3 touchdowns). Then the Giants, racked with injuries, lost four in a row and split the final four games of the season to finish 8–8. Despite the mediocre record, the Giants qualified for the play-offs but lost to the Eagles, 23-20. For the season, Eli tied for fourth in the league with 24 touchdown passes, making him the first Giants quarterback to toss 20 or more touchdowns in back-to-back seasons since Phil Simms in the mid-1980s. Eli threw 522 passes, the sixth most in Giants' history, and completed 301—a completion percentage of almost 58 percent (nearly 6 percentage points better than the previous season). However, he threw for about 500 fewer yards, 3,244, and one more interception, at 18. Meanwhile, Peyton's career continued to flourish: He led

In an NFL first, the Manning brothers faced off against each other with their respective teams, the Indianapolis Colts and the New York Giants. Peyton won this 2006 game and afterward praised his brother's performance.

the Colts to a Super Bowl victory, with a 29-17 win over the Chicago Bears.

At season's end, the Giants' star running back, Tiki Barber, retired. It was time for Eli to carry more of the load. Yet some continued to question his ability to adjust to the NFL (he's way too inconsistent and not playing like a No. 1 draft choice, his critics said) and his leadership skills (too calm). In fact, Barber,

ELI VS. PEYTON: BY THE NUMBERS

Here are statistical comparisons of Eli Manning and his brother, Peyton Manning of the Indianapolis Colts.

ELI MANNING

Regular season (through 2010)

Record as starter: 60–43

YEAR	G	COMP	ATT	PCT	YD	TD	INT	PR
2004	9	95	197	48.2	1,043	6	9	55.4
2005	16	294	557	52.8	3,762	24	17	75.9
2006	16	301	522	57.7	3,244	24	18	77.0
2007	16	297	529	56.1	3,336	23	20	73.9
2008	16	289	479	60.3	3,238	21	10	86.4
2009	16	317	509	62.3	4,021	27	14	93.1
2010	16	339	539	62.9	4,002	31	25	85.3
Total:	105	1,932	3,332	58.0	22,646	156	113	80.2

Play-offs

Record as starter: 4–3

YEAR	G	COMP	ATT	PCT	YD	TD	INT	PR
2004	(Giants did not qualify)							
2005	1	10	18	55.5	113	0	3	35.0
2006	1	16	27	59.3	161	2	1	85.6
2007	4	72	119	60.5	854	6	1	123.2
2008	1	15	29	51.7	169	0	2	40.7
2009	(Giants did not qualify)							
2010	(Giants did not qualify)							
Total:	7	113	193	57.1	1,297	8	7	77.6

PEYTON MANNING

Regular season (through 2010)

Record as starter: 131–61

YEAR	G	COMP	ATT	PCT	YD	TD	INT	PR

1998	16	326	575	56.7	3,739	26	28	71.2
1999	16	331	533	62.1	4,135	26	15	90.7
2000	16	357	571	62.5	4,413	33	15	94.7
2001	16	343	547	62.7	4,131	26	23	84.1
2002	16	392	591	66.3	4,200	27	19	88.8
2003	16	379	566	67.0	4,267	29	10	99.0
2004	16	336	497	67.6	4,557	49	10	121.1
2005	16	305	453	67.3	3,747	28	10	104.1
2006	16	362	557	65.0	4,397	31	9	101.0
2007	16	337	515	65.4	4,040	31	14	98.0
2008	16	371	555	66.8	4,002	27	12	95.0
2009	16	393	571	68.8	4,500	33	16	99.9
2010	16	450	679	66.3	4,700	33	17	91.9
Total:	208	4,682	7,210	64.9	54,828	399	198	94.9

Play-offs

Record as starter: 9–10

YEAR	G	COMP	ATT	PCT	YD	TD	INT	PR
1998	Colts did not qualify							
1999	1	19	42	45.2	227	0	0	62.3
2000	1	17	32	53.1	194	1	0	82.0
2001	Colts did not qualify							
2002	1	14	31	45.1	137	0	2	31.3
2003	3	67	103	65.0	918	9	4	106.4
2004	2	54	75	72.0	696	4	2	107.4
2005	1	22	38	57.9	290	1	0	90.9
2006	4	97	153	63.4	1,034	3	7	69.8
2007	1	33	48	68.8	402	3	2	97.7
2008	1	25	42	59.5	310	1	0	90.4
2009	3	87	128	68.0	956	6	2	99.0
2010	1	18	26	69.2	225	1	0	108.7
Total:	19	453	718	63.1	5,389	29	19	88.4

in his new job as a television football analyst, ripped on Eli's lack of fire, saying that his pep talk to the team before a game in 2006 was "comical."

Eli didn't try to change his personality, though. To get respect, he had to earn it through his performance. During the 2007 season, he got his teammates' attention by demonstrating his calm under pressure late in games. In Week 3, against the Washington Redskins, the Giants were losing 17-10 with about 12 minutes to go in the game. The team was 0–2. Another loss would have made their chances of returning to the play-offs about as slim as a pencil. Yet Eli led the team to two touchdowns and a 24-17 victory. Two weeks later, he led the team from a 24-14 third-quarter deficit to a 35-24 win over the New York Jets. Moreover, against the Chicago Bears late in the season, he rallied the Giants from a nine-point deficit in the final quarter for a 21-16 win.

Still, he was awfully inconsistent. In one game, he threw four interceptions against the Minnesota Vikings, and three of them were returned for touchdowns in a 41-17 rout at home. For the season, he ended up with almost as many interceptions, 20, as touchdown passes, 23. In a second game against Washington, he completed only 18 of 53 passes. Many experts openly wondered if Eli would ever get better. Even if he didn't, however, most people involved in the sport still considered him to be among the top 10 or 12 quarterbacks in the league. That's not bad, but was it good enough to justify being a No. 1 draft pick, or for the son of Archie Manning and the brother of Peyton?

As usual, Eli's public demeanor didn't change throughout the season, as the Giants qualified once again for the play-offs, clinching a spot as a wild-card team heading into the final game of the season with a 10–5 record. (One of those wins came against the Miami Dolphins, 13-10, in London, England—the first NFL team to win a game outside of North America.) Going into the final regular-season game, many teams in the Giants' situation would have rested their regulars to avoid injuries, but this was not just any game. It was against the New England Patriots, a team that was trying to make history. The Patriots were 15–0. One more win and they would become the first team to finish a regular season at 16–0. (The 1972 Miami Dolphins went 17–0, including the Super Bowl, after going 14–0 in the regular season.)

The Patriots were heavily favored to win, even though the contest was at Giants Stadium. The Giants, however, came to give the Patriots their best shot. Coach Tom Coughlin was playing to win. Eli had one of his best games as a pro, finishing 22 of 32 for 251 yards and 4 touchdowns. The Giants even led at one point, 28-16, but the Patriots came back to clinch their place in history by winning 38-35.

Despite the defeat, the Giants gained a lot of confidence. They had given one of the best teams ever in the NFL a big scare, and Eli produced magnificently under pressure. "We didn't win the game, but if you saw everybody in the locker room, everybody was excited," Manning said. "I never saw a locker room so upbeat after a loss because we played so well, did some good things and hung in there in a game where we didn't have to play. We wanted to. We wanted to come out and play well, and we did that."

Could the Giants use this game as a launching pad for a successful run in the play-offs?

A Super Finish

The Giants started the 2007 NFL play-offs as hardly the favorite. It was almost a given that the New England Patriots, after their undefeated regular season, would represent the AFC and then win the Super Bowl. The question was which NFC team the Patriots would face. Most experts thought that the opponent would be the Dallas Cowboys or the Green Bay Packers.

Six teams from each conference qualify for the play-offs: the four division winners and two wild-card teams. In the NFC, the wild-card teams were the Giants and the Washington Redskins, with the Cowboys, the Packers, the Seattle Seahawks, and the Tampa Bay Buccaneers as the division champs. In the AFC, the division titleholders were the Patriots, the Indianapolis Colts, the San Diego Chargers, and the Pittsburgh

Steelers. The wild-card selections were the Jacksonville Jaguars and the Tennessee Titans.

As a wild-card team, the Giants would never play a home game in the play-offs. That was fine, though. The team had actually performed better on the road (7–1) than at home (3–5) during the regular season. The Giants' first game of the play-offs was against the Buccaneers at Raymond James Stadium in Tampa Bay.

Although the Giants had a better record than the Bucs (10–6 vs. 9–7), the game wouldn't be an easy one. Eli had yet to win a play-off contest in his career, and Tampa Bay led the league in turnover/takeaway margin (more takeaways by the defense than turnovers by the offense). That wasn't good news for Manning, who tied for the NFL lead in interceptions with 20. As Eli later told a reporter, his goal was to be patient. "It was the main thing I wanted to drive home to myself. . . . You don't want to force things because the Bucs are so good at taking the ball away. You can't allow yourself to get too frustrated."

As the game started, Eli may have been too patient. The Giants didn't get a first down until the second quarter, but then the plan began to work. Throwing short, conservative passes and mixing in an effective running game, the Giants started to dominate the contest. In the fourth quarter, Eli led the team on a devastating drive, which lasted 15 plays, covered 92 yards, and took more than eight minutes off the clock. After Eli threw a four-yard touchdown pass to wide receiver Amani Toomer, the Giants led 24-7. There would be no miraculous comeback by Tampa Bay, and when the fourth quarter ended, the Giants had won their first play-off game since 2000. No one could ever say that Eli wasn't a postseason winner anymore.

In the 24-14 victory, Eli completed 20 of 27 passes for 185 yards, 2 touchdowns, and, perhaps most important, no interceptions. "Eli played smart," Tampa Bay cornerback Brian Kelly said after the game. "He made safe throws. He didn't take chances, and he didn't give us any opportunities to capitalize on mistakes because he just didn't make any."

The next game was against archrival Dallas, which had beaten the Giants twice in the regular season, 45-35 and 31-20. The Cowboys had also tied for the NFC's best record, 13–3, with the Green Bay Packers. Led by charismatic quarterback Tony Romo, the Cowboys were favored to win. But a funny thing happened on the way to the NFC Championship Game. Unlike the two regular-season contests, the Giants refused to give up long pass plays to the Cowboys. Instead, New York made Dallas grind away on offense. Eli, meanwhile, pitched two touchdown passes—4 yards and 52 yards—in the first half, which ended with the teams tied 14-14.

Dallas led 17-14 after a long drive, but New York came back to score a touchdown early in the fourth quarter on a one-yard run by running back Brandon Jacobs to lead 21-17. Dallas had one last chance, but Romo's fourth-down pass from the 22-yard line into the end zone was intercepted by Giants cornerback R.W. McQuarters with just seconds to go. The Giants had pulled off the upset, with Eli completing 12 of 18 passes for 163 yards and—again—no interceptions.

Next up, in the NFC Championship Game, were the Green Bay Packers with their legendary quarterback, Brett Favre, who had led his team to those 13 wins in the regular season and blasted the Seahawks, 42-20, in the play-offs. Favre was at the tail end of his Hall of Fame career and a sentimental favorite to return to the Super Bowl, which he won in 1996. The game would be played at fabled Lambeau Field, the scene of many great NFL games, during the infamous Wisconsin winter. The field was covered with snow and, at one point, the temperature dipped to -4° F (-20° C).

All of those factors would normally favor the Packers, but the Giants actually outplayed the home team, running 81 plays to the Packers' 49. Still, they couldn't pull away. Giants' kicker Lawrence Tynes missed two field goals, from 36 and 43 yards, in the fourth quarter, which ended with the teams tied 20-20.

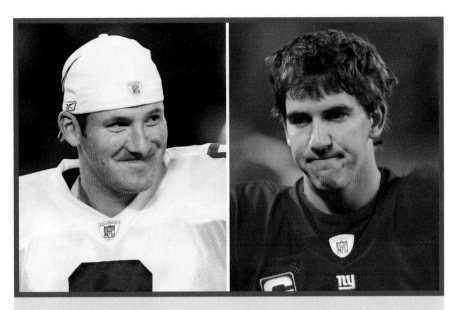

When the Giants faced the Dallas Cowboys in a 2007 NFC qualifier, Manning (*right*) faced Tony Romo (*left*), a formidable quarterback who helped his team earn a 13-3 season record. The Giants won the game and the opportunity to play the Green Bay Packers for the NFC Championship.

The game went to overtime. The first team to score would win. With the veteran Favre in charge, it appeared that the Packers had the advantage. Favre, though, made a big mistake: He threw a bad pass that was intercepted by Giants cornerback Corey Webster at Green Bay's 34-yard line. The Giants couldn't get a first down, however, and had to settle for a long field goal by Tynes, who had missed those two crucial attempts in the fourth quarter. This time, Tynes's kick from the 47-yard line flew between the uprights. The Giants pulled off one more upset, 23-20. The wild-card team that nearly no one thought had a chance was heading to the Super Bowl.

Eli had played smartly and efficiently, completing 21 of 40 passes in the terrible conditions for 254 yards and—once more—no interceptions. Eleven of those completions (for 154 yards) went to wide receiver Plaxico Burress.

"It's been about the whole team," Eli said after the game. "We've been through a lot together, and it's from coaches, players, ownership, everybody. Every sort of thing has been thrown at us, and we've handled it, I think, very well. We've made mistakes in the past, but we've learned how to deal with the media and learned how to deal when you're playing poorly or bad things happen."

THE NEW YORK GIANTS: A HISTORY

It took a long time before professional football was the most popular sport in America. When the New York Giants played their first game in October 1925, against the Frankford Yellow Jackets (a 14-0 loss), baseball, boxing, and college football were the fan favorites.

The first Giants team was owned by businessman and promoter Tim Mara. It suffered financially during the Great Depression. In 1930, he turned the Giants over to his two sons, who were extremely young. Jack Mara was 22. Wellington Mara, believe it or not, was only 14. He became the youngest owner of a football team. Wellington was a part of the ownership or leadership of the Giants for 75 years, until he died in 2005. He was inducted into the NFL Hall of Fame in 1997 for playing a key role in helping to make the league a national powerhouse.

The Giants and the NFL almost didn't survive during World War II in the 1940s. Because of the military draft, the teams used older players, and attendance dropped. Teams folded or merged. The league survived, though, and began to get stronger. Leading the way were the Giants, who produced in the 1950s such star players as Frank Gifford, Kyle Rote, Roosevelt "Rosey" Brown, and Sam Huff. The Giants remained strong through the early 1960s, playing in the NFL championship

SUPER SUNDAY

Suddenly, after a season and a career of receiving criticism, Eli was being celebrated. He had led the Giants to three straight road wins by completing a high percentage of his passes and not throwing any interceptions. The media praised his poise and decision-making. Now he had a chance to do what Peyton had done the previous season: win the Super Bowl.

game six times in eight years. Amazingly, they lost all but one of those contests (a 47-7 win over the Chicago Bears in 1956).

The Giants then floundered for about 20 years. They had bad teams and even had trouble staying in one stadium, playing in four different places. The 1980s saw a revival of the storied franchise behind such stars as quarterback Phil Simms and linebacker Lawrence Taylor. The next two decades saw the team ride through waves of success and failure. Since Eli Manning began the 2005 season as the starting quarterback, the Giants have been on another upswing.

The Giants have played in 19 NFL championship games (including 4 Super Bowls), winning 7 times. They have won three Super Bowls: in 1987, defeating the Denver Broncos 39-20; in 1991, besting the Buffalo Bills 20-19; and in 2008, beating the Patriots 17-14. Their loss came in 2001 against the Baltimore Ravens, 34-7. Perhaps their biggest game came in the 1958 NFL Championship, even though the Giants lost 23-17 in overtime to the Baltimore Colts in Yankee Stadium. It was called the Greatest Game Ever Played because of its high drama and the play of the Colts star quarterback, Johnny Unitas.

Through 2010, the team's overall record is 644–542–33 (a winning percentage of .536), and 29 players, coaches, or owners affiliated with the Giants are in the NFL Hall of Fame.

Very few people, however, thought that the Giants could do so. Despite Eli's playing and the team's outstanding defensive performances, New York seemed as if it would be one more foe for the mighty New England Patriots to conquer. The Patriots had won their two play-off games by a combined score of 52-32 to go 18–0 for the year. The undefeated 1972 Miami Dolphins were considered the greatest team ever, but if the Patriots were to win the Super Bowl, it would be hard for them not to lay claim to that distinction. They were led by quarterback Tom Brady, who had had his best season in a remarkable career by winning the MVP award and throwing a record 50 touchdown passes (breaking the mark held by Peyton). He had already won all three Super Bowls he had appeared in. The Patriots were considered a 12-point favorite.

The Giants gained a lot of confidence, however, from that 38-35 loss to the Patriots in the last game of the season. They knew they could be competitive against perhaps the best team in NFL history. The Giants had also won an amazing 10 straight games on the road—the last 7 in the regular season and 3 in the play-offs. Although the Giants' defense would certainly be tested against the highest-scoring offense in the game's history, a big key would be Eli. Could he run the Giants' offense as efficiently as he had in the play-offs? Or would he revert to the sloppy play that punctuated his regular-season performances?

The atmosphere leading up to the Super Bowl is electric and consuming. Media from all over the world descend on the site of the game (Glendale, Arizona, in this case), and demands on the time of the star players can be exhausting. Eli was a big story, and plenty was written about the turnaround in his play. Also, much attention was cast on his demeanor. Before, he had been criticized for not showing enough enthusiasm. Now, his calm approach was drawing raves.

Soon after the Green Bay victory, Eli and Peyton talked on the phone. Eli said his older brother told him that, "I am

The New England Patriots, one of the most successful and challenging football teams in the league, were considered the favorite to win the 2008 Super Bowl against the Giants. With only 1:15 left in the game, Manning threw the ball to David Tyree (*above*), who barely made the catch.

past the point where he can give me advice now; he wants it the other way around. I don't know if I believe that, but it is good to hear him say that and I will take all the advice I can get from him." The only advice Peyton wanted to give him was to try to keep his routine as normal as possible regarding off-the-field activities.

As Super Bowl XLII started on February 3, 2008, about 73,000 fans packed University of Phoenix Stadium, and an average of 97.5 million TV viewers tuned in over the course of the game—setting a record for a U.S. sporting event. After Jordin Sparks, the latest *American Idol* winner, sang the national anthem while the Blue Angels flew overhead, the game finally began.

The Giants' defense started a relentless assault on Brady. The defensive line dominated the game, sacking Brady five times and forcing him to throw the ball quicker than he would have liked. Through three quarters, both teams struggled to score, with the Patriots leading 7-3. Still, Eli was doing exactly what he and the coaching staff had wanted to do: control the ball, not make mistakes. Then, with about 11 minutes to go, Eli, after throwing a 45-yard pass to rookie tight end Kevin Boss, tossed a 4-yarder to wide receiver David Tyree to give the Giants a 10-7 lead.

The Patriot offense finally began to resemble the high-powered machine of the previous 18 games. It marched down the field, with Brady finding open receivers, until wide receiver Randy Moss hauled in a touchdown strike with only 2:42 to go.

Trailing 14-10, Eli started the next drive 83 yards away from the goal line. He led the team to New York's 44-yard line with 1:15 left. It was third down with five yards to go. Then came perhaps the greatest play in Super Bowl history. After taking the snap, Manning was almost immediately swarmed by Patriots' defensive linemen. Two New England players grasped Manning's jersey. Never known for his mobility, Manning somehow managed to keep moving and broke free, running back a few yards to his right before another Patriot came charging hard at him. He threw the ball down the middle of the field toward Tyree, who, despite his earlier touchdown catch, had contributed little during the regular season (just four receptions). As the ball floated toward him, Tyree extended his hands above his head and jumped. New England's hard-hitting safety, Rodney Harrison, leaped right with him. Tyree got his hands on the ball, but Harrison put one hand on the ball and then pulled on Tyree's right arm. Tyree pinned the ball momentarily against his helmet with one hand and, falling backward to the ground with Harrison still clutching him, managed to make the catch.

The 32-yard pass gave the Giants a first down at New England's 24-yard line. After another completion, Eli tossed a floater to the end zone from 13 yards out and Plaxico Burress made the catch for a touchdown. The Giants were in the lead, 17-14, with 35 seconds left.

Against any other team, it would seem like certain victory. Yet Brady and the Patriots still had time to get downfield for a field goal attempt to tie the game. After a sack by the Giants' Jay Alford and a desperate long pass that fell incomplete, just one second remained when New York took possession. The ball was snapped, and Eli put one knee on the ground. Game over. The New York Giants had pulled off perhaps the biggest upset in Super Bowl history. Just like his brother the year before, Eli, who completed 19 of 34 passes for 255 yards and 2 touchdowns, was named the MVP of the game.

He had had a remarkable play-off run: In 4 games, all away from home, Eli completed 72 passes in 119 attempts with only 1 interception (in the second quarter of the Super Bowl). His mother, father, and Peyton had all watched the game at the stadium. Now Eli was no longer the other Manning brother, the one who wasn't as good as Peyton. All the criticism and doubt was history. Eli Manning stood alone in the spotlight, a champion.

A Hero Is Made

After the Super Bowl win, Peyton rushed down to the Giants' locker room. He and Eli saw each other and embraced. Outside, Archie and Olivia were accepting congratulations from fans. "I remember thinking back to my days with the Saints, about fans telling me what a great day it was gonna be when I take the Saints to the Super Bowl," Archie said. "It would not have come close to the feeling you have watching your sons do what you did not do. There's nothing like it." And he got to live through two sons accomplishing the same achievement.

About the Super Bowl win, Eli said, "It was a huge deal. I've been playing sports a long time, and through high school and college I never won a championship. Never won a state championship, never won an SEC championship, never won a national championship."

Two days after bringing the Vince Lombardi Trophy back to New York City, the Giants were lauded by more than a million fans at a ticker-tape parade up a section of Broadway known as the Canyon of Heroes and later at a rally in Giants Stadium. Eli called the parade "pretty unbelievable. I'd seen other parades on TV and kind of heard about it, but going down the Canyon of Heroes and seeing the number of people who came out that day [was] unexpected."

All those complaints about Eli's lack of fire and his average-guy demeanor were now being celebrated as just the right kind of attributes to handle the fires of New York. Even *New York* magazine called him "the perfect New York hero for these times."

On playing in New York for the Giants, Manning said, "I didn't know what I was getting into. I was pretty naïve. If I knew the New York media was like this, I might have had a different idea. But I've never had any doubts or questioned my decisions about that, even the tough times. I never blamed the media for anything." Eli had come to love New York, enjoying the fast pace and the wide variety of restaurants. In fact, one of his favorite activities was to head in from his home in Hoboken, New Jersey, to try a new restaurant or go to a play on occasion.

Eli didn't seem to change because of his huge accomplishment. "I don't feel differently. Maybe someone from the outside could say something different, but I don't feel I've changed. I'm still a humble person. I still look forward to practice. I still get upset when we have bad plays. I still prepare the same way," he said. "From a football standpoint, I'm doing things the same and preparing to get better. . . . No one can take it away, but it isn't like you're finished, that you've done everything you can do. It was fun. You want to relive the experience and have that journey again. I think we have a lot more to prove. I have a lot more to prove."

A CHAMPION GETS MARRIED

Another big event happened for Eli in 2008. He and his long-time girlfriend, Abby McGrew, whom he met at the University of Mississippi, were married. "They enjoy each other the most when they're at home having a glass of wine in front of the TV," a friend once told a reporter. "They're a very low-key couple. They spend a healthy amount of time together, but they're not 24/7." Abby, who grew up in Nashville, Tennessee, worked at the time as an account executive for a company that designed evening wear and wedding gowns.

Both of Eli's brothers had had big weddings. He and Abby wanted something more intimate, with just close friends and family. In April 2008 they invited about 60 people to an exclusive resort in Cabo San Lucas, Mexico, where the Sea of Cortez meets the Pacific Ocean. The One and Only Palmilla resort has been a destination for such celebrities as Oprah Winfrey, John Travolta, Julia Roberts, George Clooney, and Cameron Diaz. A bachelor party was held the night before, with Eli the subject of a roast at one of the resort's bars. Eli also played a round of golf the day before the wedding with Peyton and friends. Ever mindful of his professional responsibilities, he stayed on his workout schedule, lifting weights in the gym. With Peyton as the best man, the couple were married at sunset in a spot with a gorgeous view of the Sea of Cortez. The reception was held atop a cliff above the beach.

ENDORSEMENTS

Because of the Super Bowl victory, Eli was suddenly a hot commodity for corporations looking for a spokesman. "When the Giants won the Super Bowl, Eli Manning jumped up to the level of his brother Peyton," said Henry Schafer, executive vice

After the Giants won the 2008 Super Bowl, New Yorkers welcomed Manning and his team home with a ticker-tape parade. Several months later, Manning married his college sweetheart, Abby McGrew, in Mexico.

president at Marketing Evaluations Inc. "He became one of the top five sports personalities out there. That shows you the power of the Super Bowl."

Eli, however, said he wanted to be careful about how many obligations he accepted. "I didn't really want to get too busy doing things," he said. "During the off-season I said, 'I've got to get four workouts in every week, and I don't want to miss any. I've made 100 percent of my workouts every year.' I don't want to have a situation where I'm doing too much off the field, where it's affecting my goals on the field. My job here is to play good football and win games for the Giants, not to do endorsements." He turned down a chance to host *Saturday Night Live*, saying he didn't want to look as if he were following in the footsteps of Peyton, who twice starred on the comedy show.

That didn't mean Eli was turning down all offers. After the Super Bowl, Eli signed on with Sears to help sell a new line of appliances. During an appearance on the ESPN program *Mike and Mike in the Morning*, he joked with the hosts about his role as a pitchman for Sears, remarking that his top skill in the kitchen was opening the refrigerator door. Eli also became a spokesman for Gatorade's new drink, G2, and did commercials for Toyota, Citizen Watch Company, and Reebok.

He also did some commercial work with his family. For Oreo, Peyton and Eli starred in an ad that said the brothers had quit the NFL to join the DSRL—the Double Stuf Racing League—to compete against each other by seeing who could lick off the icing of a double-stuffed Oreo cookie the fastest. Eli, Peyton, and Archie also wrote a children's book together called *Family Huddle*, which was published by Scholastic in 2009. (Before the Super Bowl, in 2007, Eli made a commercial for DirecTV with Peyton and his parents; when Peyton and Eli came home, their mother, Olivia, barely acknowledged them, and they found their father in the backyard coaching

rookie NFL quarterback Matt Leinart. The brothers acted as
if they were hurt. Archie said, "C'mon boys, I always wanted
a lefty.")

COMMUNITY SERVICE

Not all of Eli's off-the-field time after the Super Bowl was
spent doing endorsements, however. He volunteered for and
donated to many charitable causes. It's quite a long list, in
fact. He became the spokesman for NFL Play 60: The NFL
Movement for an Active Generation, which encourages young
people to fight off obesity by exercising for 60 minutes a day.
Eli helped raise $400,000 for Guiding Eyes for the Blind, a
nonprofit guide dog school, by acting as the host of a charity
golf tournament in Yorktown Heights, New York, the home of
the association's headquarters. He also raised money for a New
York-based drug and addiction center. Plus he was appointed
to the President's Council on Physical Fitness and Sports.

His biggest contributions were for medical care for children. Eli played a key role in opening the $2.5 million Eli
Manning Children's Clinics at the University of Mississippi
Medical Center in 2009. The clinics are a 15,600-square-foot
wing of the Blair E. Batson Hospital for Children. He was
there for the dedication of the health facility. "Touchdowns are
great," said Archie, who also was in attendance, "but this is big
stuff right here." The clinics will serve 75,000 sick Mississippi
children each year. "The state of Mississippi has been good to
me, I wanted to give back," Eli said. He became interested in
the project when he visited ill children at the Batson hospital
in 2004. He learned about the interest in adding a wing and
said, "Afterwards I told them 'I'm yours. How can we make
this happen?'"

Eli and his wife, Abby, also became involved with children's medical care in New York. They hosted a "baby ball" in
a New York restaurant to raise money for a birthing center at
St. Vincent's Hospital Manhattan. In addition, Eli also served

as the New York Division celebrity chairman for the children's nonprofit the March of Dimes.

The list of organizations he helps goes on and on: the American Heart Association, the American Red Cross, the Ronald McDonald House, the Special Olympics, the Make-A-Wish Foundation, and others. Eli's charitable work has been

HURRICANE KATRINA

In late August 2005, a huge storm was brewing in the Gulf of Mexico, heading north. Hurricanes are not uncommon in the area. Some cause a lot of damage. Others do little harm. This hurricane was called Katrina.

Like thousands of others in the region, Archie and Olivia Manning heeded the official warnings about the dangerous hurricane and evacuated their home in New Orleans to stay with Olivia's family in Philadelphia, Mississippi. Still, many people remained. Either they didn't believe the warnings or could not afford to relocate temporarily.

The storm hit on August 29 and devastated New Orleans and coastal Mississippi, resulting in about $81 billion in damages and killing an estimated 1,800 people. Flooding, caused by broken levees in New Orleans, and high winds destroyed homes and businesses. Whole neighborhoods in New Orleans were underwater. To make matters worse, the governmental relief effort was slow and disorganized, leaving survivors with hardly any food, water, or adequate shelter.

Peyton and Eli called their parents frequently as the storm arrived. Then Peyton arranged for a plane to fly to Indianapolis to load supplies. Eli flew in from New York to help. Eli, Peyton, recognized by the NFL, which sponsors an award called the Walter Payton Man of the Year. It is given to a player on each team who has done outstanding work on and off the field. Eli has won it twice (2007 and 2008) for the Giants.

As for his on-the-field accomplishments, Eli's confident play continued into the 2008 regular season. Because of the

and numerous volunteers helped load 31,000 pounds (14,000 kilograms) of bottled water, Gatorade, diapers, baby formula, blankets, pillows, and other necessities. "It's hard to watch what's happened to the city, people with no place to go, up to their waists in water. We just wanted to do something extra, so we set up this plan to help some of these people," Eli said. At first, they said they didn't want to become a burden by going to New Orleans, but they were told the victims and relief help could use the morale boost.

They flew into Baton Rouge, Louisiana. Although Archie had told them it was too dangerous to go into New Orleans, they went anyway. "They got the Red Cross or somebody to take them in," Archie said. Peyton and Eli visited shelters to talk with survivors.

Eli listened to their stories. "It was just emotional. There were a lot of sad stories, not knowing where their loved ones went. Some of the stories they had, seeing their wives and children drown right in front of them, seeing their house in ruins. It's sad, and it shows how fortunate I am for having my family. They're safe and out of there. We know where everybody is."

Super Bowl win, he was now the leader of the team. Some of the Giants' big personalities were no longer around, such as defensive end Michael Strahan (retired) and tight end Jeremy Shockey (traded). "I think that the changing of the guard was coming last year regardless of certain people still being here or not," defensive end Justin Tuck said. "He was the Super Bowl MVP, so this is definitely his team. You get the opportunity, being around him a lot, to see how he looks more comfortable, and he's realizing that now."

The Giants got off to a fast start and then got even better, winning 11 of their first 12 games. They looked as if they were a strong contender to win a second consecutive Super Bowl. Then the team stumbled after a bizarre incident involving star wide receiver Plaxico Burress. In late November, Buress went to a Manhattan nightclub with a loaded gun tucked into his waistband. At some point, the gun slipped down his leg and fired a bullet into his leg. He was not only injured, but he was also later indicted on two counts of weapon possession and one count of reckless endangerment. In 2009, he pleaded guilty to a lesser charge of attempted criminal possession of a weapon, and a judge sentenced him to two years in prison.

After the incident, the Giants still won the NFC East but lost three of their last four games to finish 12–4. Then, in the play-offs, the Philadelphia Eagles defeated the Giants, 23-11. It was a disappointing finish to a promising year, but there was still a lot to be proud of. The Giants won the NFC East for the second time in four years, with Eli as the starting quarterback. Under his leadership, the Giants had gone to the play-offs for four straight seasons (Eli had yet to play a season as the starter that the team didn't qualify for the play-offs). No other Giants quarterback had accomplished what Eli had done in each of those four seasons: more than 3,000 yards passing with 20 or more touchdowns.

In 2008, he completed 289 of 479 passes for 3,238 yards. His completion percentage of 60.3 percent was the highest of his career—as was his passer rating of 86.4. He threw 21 touchdowns and only 10 interceptions. His two best games were a 41-13 victory over St. Louis (20 of 29, 260 yards, 3 touchdowns, no interceptions) and a 44-6 win over Seattle (19 of 25, 267 yards, 2 touchdowns, no interceptions).

Football experts say that a quarterback takes about six or seven years before he really understands the game. In 2008, Eli appeared to be hitting his stride, becoming more consistent. He was rewarded for his stellar play by being named to the Pro Bowl for the first time. *The Sporting News* also named Eli its Pro Athlete of the Year for 2008. The honor was based not just on his Super Bowl win but also on his performance during the 2008 regular season, as the magazine said he was now a "great quarterback."

Before the 2009 season, Eli set another record. He signed a new contract with the Giants that made him the highest-paid player in the NFL at the time. It was a seven-year deal worth almost $107 million. The average salary of $15.27 million per year was the highest in the history of the league. (Tom Brady's deal in 2010 eclipsed that mark.) Eli was 28 years old when he signed the contract, which will last though the 2015 season. The agreement also means he's the highest-paid quarterback in the Manning family—for now. Peyton's 2004 deal with the Indianapolis Colts was for seven years and about $99 million.

"[Eli] knows how to handle pressure and he has done it before," the Giants' current general manager, Jerry Reese, said after Eli's new contract was finalized. "I don't expect to see any difference in his attitude and his work ethic. He works hard. He expects a lot from himself. He knows what his role here is with us, and we expect him to continue it for a long time."

In 2009, the Giants got off to another encouraging start, winning their first five games. Then came a trip to New Orleans to play the Saints (also undefeated). Eli's visit home didn't go well. Although the offense played well, the New York defense

Manning's success with the Giants has given him the opportunity to use his fame and fortune to help charities and social causes, such as promoting physical education in schools. Although the quarterback already owns one Super Bowl ring, he believes he has more to accomplish before he retires from football.

couldn't stop the home team, which won 48-27. That theme continued for the rest of the season as opponents racked up plenty of points.

Although Eli set career highs in yardage, completions, completion percentage, passer rating, and touchdowns, the Giants finished 8–8 and missed the play-offs for the first time since he took over as the starting quarterback.

The Giants had another streaky year in 2010, at one point winning five games in a row and reaching the halfway mark of the season with a 6–2 record. But they went 4–4 the rest of the year to finish 10–6, just missing the play-offs. The season featured the second-ever Manning Bowl, as Eli and Peyton squared off in Week 2. The Giants had no answer for the Colts, though, losing 38-14. Despite the Giants' failure to make the play-offs, Eli still rang up some good numbers, finishing with career highs in touchdowns (31), completions, attempts, and completion percentage. For the second year in a row, Manning topped 4,000 passing yards. With the good came some bad, however, as he also threw a career-high 25 interceptions, though insiders say about half of those interceptions were the fault of Manning's receivers.

By March 2011, the disappointment of the 2010 season was probably long behind him, as Abby Manning gave birth to her and Eli's first child, daughter Ava Frances. The baby, who was born on March 21, weighed in at seven pounds, four ounces.

Still, Manning's thoughts are likely never far from the football field, as he looks to get the Giants to the play-offs after a two-year drought. "We had a lot of big plays in the pass game," he said at the end of the 2010 season. "We were explosive and led the league in touchdowns over 20 yards." Yet Manning knew the offense's penchant for turnovers hurt the Giants, and he vowed to make improvements. "I put a lot on my shoulders, and I have to get better. I'm not a 25-interception quarterback. We have to fix that. That's on me, the receivers, and everybody doing that, but most of it's on me."

ELI MANNING
POSITION: **Quarterback**

FULL NAME: Elisha Nelson Manning

BORN: January 3, 1981; New Orleans, Louisiana

HEIGHT: 6'4"

WEIGHT: 225 lbs. (102 kg)

COLLEGE: **Mississippi**

TEAMS: New York Giants (2004–present)

YEAR	TEAM	G	COMP	ATT	PCT	YD	Y/A	TD	INT
2004	Giants	9	95	197	48.2	1,043	5.3	6	9
2005	Giants	16	294	557	52.8	3,762	6.8	24	17
2006	Giants	16	301	522	57.7	3,244	6.2	24	18
2007	Giants	16	297	529	56.1	3,336	6.3	23	20
2008	Giants	16	289	479	60.3	3,238	6.8	21	10
2009	Giants	16	317	509	62.3	4,021	7.9	27	14
2010	Giants	16	339	539	62.9	4,002	7.4	31	25
TOTALS:		105	1,932	3,332	58.0	22,646	6.8	156	113

RUSHING

YEAR	ATT	YD	Y/A	TD
2004	6	35	5.8	0
2005	29	80	2.8	1
2006	25	21	0.8	0
2007	29	69	2.4	1
2008	20	10	0.5	1
2009	17	65	3.8	0
2010	32	70	2.2	0
TOTALS:	158	350	2.2	3

CHRONOLOGY

1949	Archie Manning is born in Drew, Mississippi.
1971	Archie Manning marries Olivia Williams.
1974	Cooper Manning is born.
1976	Peyton Manning is born.
1980	Archie has his worst year (1–15) with the New Orleans Saints.
1981	Eli Manning is born in New Orleans.
1982	Archie Manning is traded to the Houston Oilers.
1983	Archie Manning is traded to the Minnesota Vikings.
1984	Archie Manning retires from the NFL.
1995	Eli begins to play high school football for Isidore Newman, the same school his brothers attended.
1998	Eli announces he will attend the University of Mississippi, the alma mater of his father.
2000	At a fraternity party, Eli is arrested and charged with public drunkenness.
2001	After redshirting one season and sitting on the bench for another, Eli wins the starting quarterback position for Ole Miss as a sophomore.
2004	Eli leads Mississippi to its first major bowl victory in 34 years, defeating Oklahoma State 31-28 in the Cotton Bowl.
	The San Diego Chargers choose Eli as the No. 1 pick in the NFL Draft; he is then traded to the New York Giants.
	Eli becomes the starting quarterback in the ninth game of the season for the Giants; the team loses six straight games before winning the last contest of the season against the Dallas Cowboys.

2006   Peyton and Eli face off for the first time in their careers, with Peyton's team coming out on top, 26-21.

2007   The NFL selects Eli as the Giants representative for the Walter Payton Man of the Year award (for outstanding work on and off the field). Eli earns the same honor in 2008.

2008   Following the 2007 regular season, the New York Giants win the Super Bowl over the New England Patriots, 17-14. Eli is named MVP of the game.

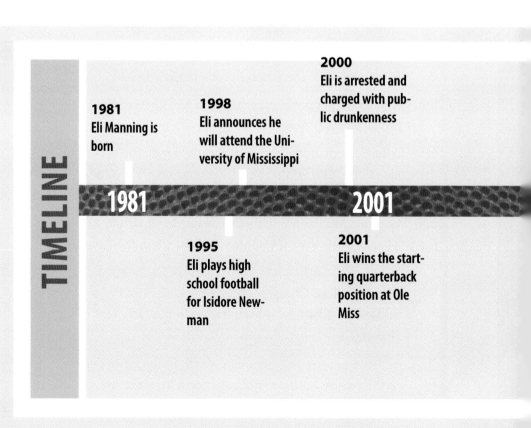

TIMELINE

1981
Eli Manning is born

1998
Eli announces he will attend the University of Mississippi

2000
Eli is arrested and charged with public drunkenness

1981

2001

1995
Eli plays high school football for Isidore Newman

2001
Eli wins the starting quarterback position at Ole Miss

In Mexico, Eli marries his college girlfriend, Abby McGrew.

Eli is selected to the Pro Bowl for the first time; *The Sporting News* names Eli as its Pro Athlete of the Year after the 2008 regular season.

2009   Eli is awarded a seven-year, $107 million contract, making him the highest-paid player in the history of the NFL at the time.

2011   Eli and Abby Manning's first child, daughter Ava Frances, is born.

2006
Peyton and Eli face off for the first time in their careers, with Peyton's team winning

2008
Giants win the Super Bowl over the New England Patriots; Eli is named MVP of the game and is selected to the Pro Bowl for the first time

2004

2009

ELI MANNING

2004
Eli is chosen as the No. 1 NFL Draft pick, then becomes the starting quarterback in the ninth game of the season for the Giants

2007
Eli is selected as the Giants representative for the Walter Payton Man of the Year award

2009
Eli becomes the highest-paid player in the NFL

GLOSSARY

American Football Conference (AFC)   One of the two conferences in the National Football League. The AFC was established after the NFL merged with the American Football League (AFL) in 1970.

blitz   In this defensive play, the linebackers or defensive backs charge into the offensive team's backfield to sack the quarterback.

bowl game   A game played by college football teams after the regular season. It is considered a reward for a successful season. Some of the more famous bowl games are the Rose Bowl, the Sugar Bowl, and the Fiesta Bowl.

center   The offensive player who snaps the ball to the quarterback.

combine   An audition of college football players by NFL teams before the NFL Draft.

cornerback   A defensive back who lines up near the line of scrimmage across from a wide receiver. The cornerback's primary job is to disrupt passing routes, to defend against short and medium passes in the passing game, and to contain the rusher on rushing plays.

defensive backs   The cornerbacks or safeties on the defensive team. Their primary goal is to prevent receivers from catching passes.

draft   The selection of collegiate players for entrance into the National Football League. Typically, the team with the worst record in the previous season picks first in the draft.

drive   A series of plays by the offensive team that can lead to a touchdown or a field goal.

end zone   The area between the end line and the goal line, bounded by the sidelines.

field goal   A three-point score made when a placekicker kicks the ball through the uprights of the opponent's goal.

first down   The first of a set of four downs. Usually, a team that has a first down needs to advance the ball 10 yards to receive another first down, but penalties or field position (i.e., fewer than 10 yards from the opposing end zone) can affect this.

fourth down   The final of a set of four downs. Unless a first down is achieved or a penalty forces a replay of the down, the team will lose control of the ball after this play. If a team does not think it can get a first down, it will often punt on fourth down or kick a field goal if close enough to do so.

fullback   An offensive player who lines up in the backfield and is generally responsible for blocking for the running back or quarterback. The fullback may also be used as a short-yardage runner.

fumble   When an offensive player loses control of the football that he is carrying.

goal line   The line at the front of the end zone. A touchdown is scored when the football breaks the plane of the goal line.

guard   A position on the offensive line on both sides of the center (there are two guards on an offensive line). Their jobs are to block downfield on running plays and protect the quarterback on passing plays.

handoff   When a player gives the ball to a teammate in back of or beside him, instead of passing it forward.

Heisman Trophy   An award presented annually to the most outstanding player in college football.

huddle   When teammates gather to discuss the next play.

incomplete pass   A forward pass that a player does not catch.

interception   A pass that is caught by a defensive player, giving his team the ball.

kickoff   The kick that begins a game, the second half, or overtime, or that follows a touchdown or field goal.

line of scrimmage   The imaginary line that stretches across the field and separates the two teams before the snap; before a play, teams line up on either side of the line of scrimmage.

linebacker   A position on defense. Linebackers typically play one to six yards behind the defensive linemen. Most defenses use either three or four linebackers.

National Football Conference (NFC)   One of two conferences in the National Football League. The NFC was established after the NFL merged with the American Football League (AFL) in 1970.

pass interference   An illegal play by a defender in which he tries to prevent a receiver from catching the ball.

passer rating   A system used to gauge the effectiveness of a quarterback.

pocket   The area of protection for the quarterback that is formed by the offensive line when he drops back to pass.

punt   A kick in which the ball is dropped and kicked before it reaches the ground. A punt usually occurs on fourth down and is designed to drive the opposing team as far back as possible before it takes possession of the ball.

quarterback   The player who directs the offense for his football team.

reception   A caught pass.

redshirt   A term used in college football. It means that a player is still on the team but can't play that season. It's a way for young players to learn the complex college game and not lose a year of eligibility.

running back   An offensive player who runs with the football; also known as a tailback, halfback, or fullback.

sack   Any tackle of a quarterback by the defense behind the line of scrimmage. A sack also occurs if a defensive player forces the offense to fumble the ball out of bounds behind the scrimmage line.

safety   A defensive player who lines up in the secondary but often deeper than the cornerbacks. A safety is also a two-point score that occurs by downing an opposing ball carrier in his own end zone.

scramble   A run by the quarterback out of the pocket while his receivers try to get open. The quarterback will run until he can attempt a pass or rush for yardage himself.

screen pass   A forward pass to a receiver at or behind the line of scrimmage; the receiver is protected by a screen of blockers.

secondary   The defensive players who line up behind the linebackers and defend the pass.

sidelines   The lines marking out of bounds on each side of a football field.

signing bonus   An extra amount of money that a player receives when he signs a contract to play for a team.

snap   The handoff from the center, usually to the quarterback, to start a play.

sudden death   An overtime game in which the team that scores first wins.

Super Bowl   The championship game of the NFL, pitting the champions of the AFC and the NFC against each other.

tackle   To stop the player with the ball and bring him to the ground. Also a position on the offensive line next to the guards (there are two tackles on an offensive line). Their jobs are to block downfield on running plays and protect the quarterback on passing plays.

tight end   An offensive player who lines up on the line of scrimmage next to a tackle. Tight ends are used as blockers during running plays and either run a route or stay in to block during passing plays.

time-out   A break in action requested by either team or one of the officials. In the NFL, each team gets three time-outs per half. The clock is stopped for a time-out.

touchdown   A play worth six points in which any part of the ball while legally in the possession of a player crosses the plane of the opponent's goal line. A touchdown allows the team a chance for one extra point by kicking the ball or two points by running or passing the ball into the end zone.

two-point conversion   A scoring play after a touchdown during which a team can add two points to the score instead of kicking for just one point; in a two-point conversion, the scoring team has one play to run or pass the ball into the end zone from the opponent's two-yard line.

wide receiver   An offensive player who runs a passing route downfield.

wild card   A team that does not win a division title but has the next best record in the conference. In each conference, two wild-card teams make the play-offs.

Wonderlic   An intelligence test given to prospective NFL players.

BIBLIOGRAPHY

Altobelli, Lisa. "Life On and Off the Field." *Sports Illustrated*, October 11, 2004.

Attner, Paul. "The First Family." *The Sporting News*, March 22, 2004.

Banks, Don. "Best Quarterback Class Ever?" SI.com, August 28, 2009.

Bell, Jarrett. "Manning Brothers, Other NFL Players Lend Hand." *USA Today*, September 6, 2005.

Blaudschun, Mark. "College Football 2001." *Boston Globe*, August 31, 2001.

———. "Manning Looks Like a Throwback." *Boston Globe*, April 17, 2004.

Bondy, Filip. "Eli's Coming." *Daily News* (New York), September 21, 1997.

———. "Outcome All Relative." *Daily News* (New York), September 11, 2006.

Chadiha, Jeffri. "What a Manning Wants." *Sports Illustrated*, May 3, 2004.

Clayton, John. "Cold Reality: Burress Couldn't Be Stopped." ESPN.com, January 20, 2008.

Crouse, Karen. "Eli Manning Took Cues from Mother." *New York Times*, January 29, 2008.

Dellenger, Ross. "Eli Does 'Big Stuff' for UMC." Clarionledger. com (Jackson, Mississippi), June 27, 2009.

DeShazier, John. "Eli Manning Is as Good as Advertised." *Times-Picayune* (New Orleans), October 28, 2001.

Drape, Joe. "College Football: Eli Manning Inherits the Reins at Ole Miss." *New York Times*, October 19, 2001.

Dulac, Gerry. "Quarterback Class of 2004 Chasing '83 Picks." *Pittsburgh Post-Gazette*, October 4, 2009.

Duncan, Jeff. "New York Media Have a Field Day with Manning." *Times-Picayune* (New Orleans), July 10, 2004.

Finney, Peter. "Manning Boys Set to Throw for Real." *Times-Picayune* (New Orleans), July 12, 1998.

——. "Eli Still Learning Way Around." *Times-Picayune* (New Orleans), March 2, 2005.

——. "Mom's Big Night." *Times-Picayune* (New Orleans), September 8, 2006.

——. "Proud Papa Archie Still Glows Over 2007, '08," *Times-Picayune* (New Orleans), August 31, 2008.

Foster, Mary. "All in the Family." *The Advocate* (Baton Rouge), November 25, 1997.

Garcia, Julian. "Brothers Still Talking." *Daily News* (New York), September 8, 2006.

Gildea, William. "At Ole Miss, Passing the Torch." *Washington Post*, August 4, 2002.

Greenberg, Steve. "SN 2008 Pro Athlete of the Year." *The Sporting News*, December 22, 2008.

Hack, Damon. "This Manning Brother Lets Arm Do the Talking." *New York Times*, April 24, 2004.

Kalec, William. "Mannings Manage Eli's Hype." *Times-Picayune.* (New Orleans), July 12, 2003.

Korth, Joanne. "Eli Becomes His Own Manning." *St. Petersburg Times*, November 22, 2001.

Kram, Mark. "A Lineup That Sells." *Philadelphia* (PA) *Daily News,* March 30, 2009.

Jenkins, Lee. "Chargers Defy Skeptics, Especially the Mannings." *New York Times*, December 26, 2004.

Lagarde, Dave. "Continuing a Football Legacy." *Times-Picayune* (New Orleans), September 16, 1995.

———. "Manning's Decision a Mystery." *Times-Picayune* (New Orleans), January 12, 2003.

———. "Manning Returned for 'One More Shot.'" *Times-Picayune* (New Orleans), November 20, 2003.

Lewis, Michael. "The Eli Experiment." *New York Times*, December 19, 2004.

McLaughlin, Eliot C. "Lawyers, Insurance Firms Cash in on Fantasy Football." CNN.com, September 10, 2009.

Muske, Mark. "Shouldering a Giant Load." *Washington Post*, November 30, 2004.

Myers, Gary. "Archie to S.D.: Hands Off Eli." *Daily News* (New York), April 22, 2004.

———. "Eli Shouldn't Start Too Soon." *Daily News* (New York), April 26, 2004.

———. "Eli Aims to Inflict Giant Payback on Peyton." *Daily News* (New York), September 4, 2006.

"Nation's Top 100 Seniors." *Sun-Times* (Chicago), August 21, 1998.

Pasquarelli, Len. "Poised, Patient Manning Delivers for Giants." ESPN.com, January 6, 2008.

Patton, Gregg. "Eli Sucks It Up Before a Hostile San Diego Crowd." *Press Enterprise* (Riverside, California), September 27, 2005.

Peck, Renée. "The Mannings at Home." *Times-Picayune* (New Orleans), December 9, 2006.

Piazza, Jo, and Hutchinson, Bill. "Catch of the Day." *Daily News* (New York), April 19, 2008.

———. "Eli Calls Mystery H'moon Audible." *Daily News* (New York), April 21, 2008.

Quinn, T.J. "Proud Papa." *Daily News* (New York), January 8, 2006.

Reid, John. "Manning Passes Newman by Fisher, 34-24." *Times-Picayune* (New Orleans), October 19, 1996.

———. "To the Last Manning." *Times-Picayune* (New Orleans), September 3, 1998.

———. "Manning Follows His Heart to Join Cutcliffe at Ole Miss." *Times-Picayune* (New Orleans), December 19, 1998.

"Serena Tops Venus in Straight-sets Final." Associated Press, July 4, 2009.

Serby, Steve. "Way to Go Bro." *New York Post*, February 4, 2007.

Smith, Stephen A. "Sometimes Father Really Does Know Best." *Philadelphia Inquirer*, April 25, 2004.

Sternbergh, Adam. "Underdog." *New York*, January 27, 2008.

Talbot, Chris. " 'First Family' of Football Lauded." Associated Press, March 18, 2009.

"The History of Fantasy Football." Fantasyfootballinstitute.com, July 16, 2008.

Thompson, Wright. "North Toward Home." *Times-Picayune* (New Orleans), October 23, 2001.

Triplett, Mike. "Rebels' Manning Remains Low Key." *Times-Picayune* (New Orleans), July 31, 2003.

Vacchiano, Ralph. "Passing Grade on Eli's Elbow." *Daily News* (New York), August 23, 2005.

———. "Disaster Hits Home for Eli." *Daily News* (New York), September 6, 2005.

———. "Giants Make Eli Manning Richest Quarterback in NFL." *Daily News* (New York), August 5, 2009.

Walton, Marsha. "Manning Brothers Team Up for Katrina Relief." CNN.com, September 5, 2005.

Wassink, Zac. "Eli Manning Is a Sandwich." Examiner.com, July 17, 2009.

Weisman, Larry. " 'I Have a Lot More to Prove.' " *USA Today*, August 15, 2008.

Whiteside, Kelly. "Eli at Ease Being a Manning." *USA Today*, October 4, 2002.

Whittaker, Rachel. "Athletes Arrive at Manning Camp." Daily-comet.com, July 10, 2009.

Wilner, Barry. "Patriots Rewrite Record Books." Associated Press, December 30, 2007.

Yorio, Kara. "Eli's Coming." *The Sporting News*, December 9, 2005.

FURTHER READING

Christopher, Matt. *On the Field with . . . Peyton and Eli Manning*. New York: Little, Brown, 2008.

Manning, Archie and Peyton, with John Underwood. *Manning*. New York: HarperEntertainment, 2001.

Vacchiano, Ralph. *Eli Manning: The Making of a Quarterback*. New York: Skyhorse Publishing, 2008.

WEB SITES

New York Giants Media Guide
http://www.giants.com/mediaguide/contents.html

Player: Eli Manning
http://www.giants.com/team/player34.html

Profile: Eli Manning
http://sports.espn.go.com/nfl/players/profile?playerId=5526

Profile: Eli Manning
http://www.nfl.com/players/elimanning/profile?id=MAN473170

Stats: Eli Manning
http://sportsillustrated.cnn.com/football/nfl/players/6760/

Super Bowl XLII
http://www.nfl.com/superbowl/42

PICTURE CREDITS

INDEX

A

Accorsi, Ernie, 46, 54
AFC. *See* American Football Conference
Aikman, Troy, 47
Alabama University, 37, 40
Alford, Jay, 75
All-Pro, 16
American Football Conference (AFC), 52, 56, 66
antiques, 10, 20–21
Arizona Cardinals, 55
Arkansas State University, 40
Atlanta Falcons
  games against, 21, 49, 52
Auburn University, 40

B

Baltimore Ravens, 71
Barber, Tiki, 54, 57, 61, 64
Bart Starr Humanitarian Award, 17
Bauer, Hank, 56
Blackledge, Todd, 50
Bledsoe, Drew, 29
Bradford, Sam, 21
Brady, Tom, 52, 85
  and the Super Bowl, 72, 74–75
Brandt, Gil, 47
Brees, Drew, 56
Brown, Roosevelt, 70
Buffalo Bills, 50, 71
Burress, Plaxico, 57, 69, 75, 84
Byron "Whizzer" White Humanitarian Award, 17

C

Carolina Panthers, 55, 57
Chicago Bears, 25, 61, 71
  games against, 64
childhood, 14, 18
  and his mother, 21–23
  and sports, 19–21

civil rights
  riots and murders, 14–15
  and segregation, 14
Cleveland Browns, 47
Clooney, George, 78
Collins, Kerry, 49
community service
  and Hurricane Katrina, 82–83
  work with kids, 13, 81–82
Condon, Tom, 45
Cotton Bowl, 42
Coughlin, Tom
  coach, 49, 65
Cutcliffe, David
  college coach, 31, 34, 36–37

D

Dallas Cowboys, 47, 66
  games against, 53–54, 56, 68
Denver Broncos, 47, 50, 71
  games against, 56–57
Diaz, Cameron, 78
Dorsey, John, 44
Drew, Mississippi, 14

E

Eason, Tony, 50
education
  college, 10–11, 21, 29–36
  high school, 9–10, 24, 26–30
Egan, Merrick, 49–50
Elway, John, 47–48, 50–51
endorsements, 13, 78
  contracts, 46, 80
  DirectTV, 80–81

F

Family Huddle (children's book), 80
fantasy football, 38
Faulkner, William, 11
Favre, Brett, 20, 68–69
Florida State University, 40

G

Gibson, Althea, 30
Gifford, Frank, 70
Gilbride, Kevin, 57
Gonzales, Anthony, 21
Green Bay Packers, 44, 66
    games against, 68–69, 72
Guiding Eyes for the Blind,
    81

H

Harrison, Marvin, 21
Harrison, Rodney, 74–75
Heisman Trophy, 15, 21, 25, 37,
    40, 42
Hoboken, New Jersey
    living in, 11, 13, 20, 77
Houston Oilers, 8, 16, 19
Howorth, Richard, 34
Huff, Sam, 70
Hurricane Katrina, 82–83

I

Independence Bowl, 39
Indianapolis Colts, 66
    games against, 58–60, 86
    and Peyton, 8, 21, 25, 47,
        58–63, 85–86
    and the Super Bowl, 8, 61
injuries, 39, 55
Isidore Newman
    football at, 10, 24–28
    records and awards at,
        25, 28

J

Jacksonville Jaguars, 67
Jacobs, Brandon, 68

K

Kansas City Chiefs, 50
Kelly, Brian, 67
Kelly, Jim, 50–51

L

Lambert, Jack, 48
Leftwich, Byron, 39
Leinart, Matt, 81
Lemming, Tom, 28
Losman, J.P., 45, 50–51
Louisiana State, 37, 42

M

Manning, Abby McGrew (wife),
    13, 78, 81, 87
Manning, Archie (father), 10, 20,
    23, 28, 35, 39, 49–50, 59–60,
    82–83
    charity work, 17
    draft controversy, 45–47
    Eli compared to, 8–9, 32, 37,
        64
    endorsements, 80–81
    and football, 8, 10–11, 14–16,
        19, 21, 24–29, 31, 33–34,
        36–37, 40, 42–43, 76
    marriage, 16, 19
    parents, 15
    retirement from football, 16,
        18
Manning, Ava Frances (daugh-
    ter), 87
Manning, Cooper (brother),
    29
    business, 25
    childhood, 18–19
    education, 10–11, 21, 24–25,
        31
    and football, 8, 10, 19, 24–26
    health problems, 8, 24–25
Manning, Peyton (brother), 30,
    49, 76, 78, 82–83
    advice, 72–73
    awards, 25, 59
    childhood, 18–19
    and the Colts, 8, 21, 25, 47, 52,
        58–63, 85–86

education, 10, 21, 24–25, 28, 31

Eli compared to, 8–11, 28–29, 32, 34, 37, 42, 44–45, 59, 62–64, 75, 80

endorsements, 80–81

and football, 8–10, 19–20, 24–28, 37, 40, 42–43, 52, 58–61, 85–86

and the Super Bowl, 8, 25, 61

Manning, Olivia (mother), 10, 59, 76, 80, 82

childhood, 22–23

Eli's relationship with, 8–9, 11, 18, 20, 22–23, 27

marriage, 16, 19

Manning Passing Academy, 21

Mara, Jack, 70

Mara, Tim, 70

Mara, Wellington, 70

March of Dimes, 82

Marino, Dan, 50–51

marriage, 13, 78

Marshall University, 39

McCoy, Colt, 21

McLeod, Scott, 10

McQuarters, R.W., 68

media, 27, 56

aggressive, 11, 48–49

attention, 9, 57, 59, 70

criticism of, 8, 13, 46, 61, 71–72, 75, 77

demand, 51

press conferences, 34

Memphis State University, 40

Miami Dolphins, 50, 72

games against, 64–65

Miami University, 45

Mike and Mike in the Morning, 80

Minnesota Vikings, 8, 16

games against, 57, 64

Mirnyi, Max, 30

Mississippi State, 39

Montgomery, James, 50

Moss, Randy, 74

Murray, Bill, 20

Music City Bowl, 36

N

Nashville, Tennessee, 36, 78

National Football Conference (NFC), 66, 84

championship game, 57, 68

records, 68

National Football Foundation and College Hall of Fame, 42

National Football League (NFL), 7, 19–20, 38, 43

drafts, 11, 16, 25, 39, 44–47, 50–52, 56, 61, 64

fans, 8, 11, 13, 46–47, 56–57, 73, 76

history, 52, 59, 70, 72, 85

MVP, 16, 25

play-offs, 45, 57, 60, 64–69, 72, 84, 86–87

Pro Days, 44–45

scouts, 44

stars, 8, 13, 28–29, 47, 81

Wonderlic, 45

National Guard, 14

New England Patriots, 16, 50, 52, 66, 71

games against, 7–8, 13, 65

and the Super Bowl, 7, 13, 72–75

New Orleans, 82–83

growing up in, 8–9, 11, 14, 18, 20, 24, 28

New Orleans Saints, 8, 16, 44, 76

games against, 55, 85–86

New York Giants

2004 draft, 46–47, 50

contracts with, 13, 51, 85

fans, 8, 11, 13, 47, 51–52, 56, 77

history of, 47, 57, 60, 70–71

locker room, 8
playing for, 7–8, 11–13, 21,
    44–87
play-offs, 13, 57, 60, 64–69, 84,
    86–87
rookie year, 13, 47–54
and the Super Bowl, 7–8, 13,
    49, 72–78, 84
teammates, 49, 52, 54, 56–57,
    59, 61, 64–65, 68–70, 72,
    74–75, 84–85
trade to, 11
New York Jets, 50, 64
NFC. *See* National Football
    Conference
NFL Play 60: The NFL Move-
    ment for an Active Generation,
    81
NFL. See National Football
    League
Nicholls State University, 21
Nixon, Richard, 34
North Carolina State, 45, 47

O

Oakland Raiders, 38
O'Brien, Ken, 50
Oklahoma State University, 42
Oxford, Mississippi, 11, 13, 40,
    42
    economic boost in, 33–34

P

Parks, Dave, 21
Paterno, Joe, 29
Penn State University, 29
Peppers, Julius, 55
personality, 8, 18, 28–29, 59, 64,
    77
Philadelphia Eagles
    games against, 52, 60, 84
Philadelphia, Mississippi, 22, 82
Pittsburgh Steelers, 50–51,
    66–67

Plunkett, Jim, 16
President's Council on Physical
    Fitness and Sports, 81
Price, Mike, 29
Pro Bowl, 13, 50, 85

Q

quarterbacks, 7, 19, 38, 45
    best, 11, 15–16, 20, 25, 27, 36,
        40, 42, 50–52, 85
    camps, 21
    fumbles, 26, 49, 60
    inconsistency, 8, 13, 61, 64, 85
    interceptions, 8, 13, 28, 36–37,
        39–40, 47, 52, 54, 57, 60, 64,
        67–69, 71, 85, 87
    rookie, 47, 49–51
    starting, 36, 46, 49–50, 55, 59,
        71, 84, 86

R

Reese, Jerry, 85
Rivers, Philip, 45, 47, 50–51
Roberts, Julia, 78
Roethlisberger, Ben, 45, 50–51
Romo, Tony, 68
Rote, Kyle, 70
Rushing, Tom, 28

S

San Diego Chargers, 11, 66
    2004 draft, 45–47, 50
    games against, 56
Sansing, David, 15
Schafer, Henry, 78, 80
Seattle Seahawks, 66
    games against, 85
SEC. *See* Southeastern Confer-
    ence
Shockey, Jeremy, 21, 84
Shreveport, Louisiana, 39
Simms, Phil, 60, 71
Smith, A.J., 45–46
South Carolina University, 40

Southeastern Conference (SEC), 11, 20, 25, 37, 39, 77
    Academic Honor Roll, 21
    history, 42
    rivals, 40
Sparks, Jordin, 73
Sporting News, 85
Sports Illustrated, 57
Stanford University, 16
St. Louis Rams
    games against, 85
Strahan, Michael, 84
Sugar Bowl, 34, 42
Super Bowl, 46, 65–66, 68–69, 80–81
    champions, 7, 77
    history, 7, 75
    MVP, 8, 25, 75, 84
    playing in, 7–8, 13
    upsets, 7
    winning, 7–8, 13, 20, 49–51, 61, 71–78, 84–85
    XLII, 7–8, 13, 73–75

T
Tagliabue, Paul, 46
Tampa Bay Buccaneers, 66
    games against, 67
Tarkenton, Fran, 57
Taylor, Lawrence, 71
Tennessee Titans, 67
Thibodaux, Louisiana, 21
Tomlinson, LaDainian, 56
Toomer, Amani, 57
Travolta, John, 78
Tuck, Justin, 84
Tulane University, 45
Tynes, Lawrence, 68–69
Tyree, David, 7, 74–75

U
Unitas, Johnny, 71
University of Florida, 25

University of Mississippi, 8, 18, 21, 25, 78
    Archie at, 10, 14–16, 24, 31–34, 36, 42
    awards at, 42
    Eli Manning Children's Clinics at, 81
    fans, 10, 31, 36–37
    football at, 10–11, 14–16, 24, 30–31, 33–34, 36–37, 39–40, 42
    public drunkenness at, 35
    records at, 11, 15
    redshirted at, 34, 36
    riots at, 14–15
    Walk of Champions, 10–11
University of Southern California, 39
University of Tennessee, 10, 15, 25, 31, 42
University of Texas, 31
University of Virginia, 31

V
Vaught, John, 36

W
Walter Payton Man of the Year award, 83
Warner, Kurt, 49, 52
Washington Redskins, 66
    games against, 53, 64
Washington State, 29
Webster, Corey, 69
West Virginia University, 36
White, Jason, 42
Williams, Richard, 30
Williams, Serena, 30–31
Williams, Venus, 30–31
Winfrey, Oprah, 78
Winkenbach, Bill, 38
Winslow, Kellen, 47
World War II, 70

ABOUT THE AUTHOR

RAY PAPROCKI, the editor of *Columbus Monthly* magazine, has won more than 35 journalism awards. He has coauthored with his wife, Sherry Beck Paprocki, *The Complete Idiot's Guide to Branding Yourself.* A former stringer for the *Wall Street Journal,* he has written freelance articles for the *Chicago Tribune,* the Cleveland *Plain Dealer Sunday Magazine, Internet Retailer, The Sporting News,* and *Denison Magazine,* among others. He has written five children's publications and authored a book of personal essays, *A Columbus State of Mind.* A graduate of the Ohio State School of Journalism, Paprocki has taught as an adjunct professor at Otterbein and Capital universities. He is married with two adult children and lives near Columbus, Ohio.